the beerbistro cookbook

THE
beerbistro
COOKBOOK

by Stephen Beaumont and Brian Morin

KEY PORTER BOOKS

Library and Archives Canada Cataloguing in Publication

Beaumont, Stephen, 1964-
    Beerbistro cookbook / Stephen Beaumont, Brian Morin.

ISBN 978-1-55470-140-7

    1. Cookery (Beer). 2. Beer. I. Morin, Brian II. Title.
TX726.3.B434 2009   641.6'23   C2008-906940-4

The publisher gratefully acknowledges the support of the Canada Council for the Arts and the Ontario Arts Council for its publishing program. We acknowledge the support of the Government of Ontario through the Ontario Media Development Corporation's Ontario Book Initiative.

We acknowledge the financial support of the Government of Canada through the Book Publishing Industry Development Program (BPIDP) for our publishing activities.

Key Porter Books Limited
Six Adelaide Street East, Tenth Floor
Toronto, Ontario
Canada M5C 1H6

www.keyporter.com

Text design and electronic formatting: Alison Carr
Photography by Mike McColl

Printed and bound in Canada

09 10 11 12 13 5 4 3 2 1

dedication

From Brian: Thank you, Mom, for your cooking; Alison, Julianne, and Kath for supporting and believing in my dreams; and all the staff of beerbistro, because without your dedication, beerbistro would never be what it is today.

From Stephen: I'd like to dedicate this book to all the members of the beerbistro staff and management team, past and present, who have embraced the world of beer with enthusiasm and dedication— it's your efforts that make us look good. I'd also like to send a special word of thanks and appreciation to Dayna, queen of the bar, who has not only become one of the more beer-savvy people I know, but also understands those times when the occasion is more important than the beer.

contents

welcome to beerbistro

There exists in the heart of downtown Toronto, steps from the financial district and minutes from the big theatres, a place that's just a little bit different. Part bar and part restaurant, it's where beer is not only respected but also celebrated, and where ales and lagers belong not just at the bar but at the table and, most importantly, in the kitchen.

This place is beerbistro.

When we opened beerbistro in the fall of 2003, we understood that it would take a while to catch on, and sure enough, it did. People weren't sure what to make of a bar that took its food seriously, and were even more confused about a restaurant that paid attention to its beer. In a city where the craft beer renaissance had been in full bloom for nearly two decades but still hadn't quite caught fire the way it had in other parts of North America, drinkers and diners alike were a bit baffled by the idea of not just drinking beer but eating it too.

But perhaps we're getting a little ahead of ourselves. There's still a matter of how we got to that opening.

Having met and forged a friendship some years earlier, the two of us were of the same mind when it came to beer, viewing it as not only an astoundingly diverse and complex drink, but also a beverage deserving of much greater culinary respect than it had been receiving. If people could get all excited about the different ways various salts could influence their food, Brian wondered, why aren't chefs at least as excited about the far, far wider and more diverse palette of flavours to be found within the world of beer?

And so Brian formed a vision that was as elemental as it was inspired: Create a casual restaurant where beer both flavours the food and enhances the dining experience at the table. Make it a comfortable place, but not at all a pub, and feature cuisine drawn from all corners of Toronto's multicultural mosaic. Keep prices reasonable, service levels high, and make sure that everyone—customers, staff, and management included—has a good time.

Steve signed on as the beer wrangler almost immediately, and together we set out to develop a place where the kitchen would make full use of all the world's great ales and lagers, from bone-dry lambics to rich and malty Belgian ales, roasty and imposing Imperial stouts to lean and crisp Pilsners, and citrusy American pale ales to clove-accented hefeweizens. If there's a beer to be had with a flavour that's worthy, Steve would find it and Brian would put it to use.

It's called beer cuisine.

Of course, beerbistro wasn't the first place to feature beer cuisine. The northern French and Belgians have long since developed their own cuisine *à la bière* dating back centuries, and the British, Germans, and Czechs had been making use of their national ales and lagers for generations, although mostly in isolated dishes rather than as the basis for a kitchen philosophy. In fact, it's quite likely that for as long as there have been beer and cooking, there has been some form of beer cuisine, whether it's marinating meat in ale or flavouring soup with spiced beer.

The idea behind beerbistro, however, is a little different. Being based in multicultural Toronto, the gastronomic world quite literally sits on our doorstep, with Little Italy to the west, Greektown to the east, Chinatowns on either side, and Little Portugals, Indias, Koreas, Polands, and almost any other nation you can think of scattered in between. Our goal, then, was and is to incorporate beer into a diverse, multi-ethnic menu that is as approachable as it is delectable, as comforting as it is captivating.

But still beer cuisine.

At its most basic, beer cuisine is any dish that uses beer in its creation, from ale-fuelled chili to foie gras pâté spiced with blonde Belgian ale. If you've ever marinated flank steak in ale, or steamed mussels in wheat beer, or made beer bread from one of those kits sold in specialty food stores, you too have created beer cuisine. Instead of using beer where it seems logical, Brian and his staff go out of their way to develop new and delicious ways to highlight the myriad flavours found in the taps and bottles at beerbistro.

But the cuisine at beerbistro is about more than just beer. Equally important to us is the ethic of cooking from scratch, whether that means baking our own bread, curing and smoking our own bacon, or churning up our unique selection of beer ice creams, also known as Beerscreams. This allows us full control over virtually everything that appears on a plate at the restaurant, and also means that there's never a dull moment in the beerbistro kitchen.

When we opened beerbistro, we decided on two supremely compatible but certainly distinct mandates. On the bar and beverage side, we wanted to change the way people think about beer. In this, of course, we mean to take beer from the ice-cold thirst quencher

role it so often fills and place it instead at the table, as a wonderful accent to a meal, both in the food and, equally, in the glass beside the food. Ideally, we wanted people to walk away from beerbistro with what we call a Beer Experience, during which their understanding of beer as a beverage has fundamentally changed.

On the kitchen side, we desired to both celebrate and elevate fresh-market beer cuisine, employing the vast diversity of flavours found in beer to craft new tastes and food experiences, whether in a salad vinaigrette, a foie gras mousse, or a simple grilled hamburger. In this, we would not only give our customers unique food experiences to go with their beer experiences, but also excite and challenge our kitchen staff, inviting each and every one of them—from sous-chef to dishwasher—along on this funky ride of beer cuisine discovery.

We believe we've been successful on both fronts, which is the reason you're holding this cookbook in your hands.

As we noted earlier, it took people a little while to catch on to what we were doing, but catch on they did. Five years after that opening day, beerbistro has become a success beyond our early imaginings, serving up a varied seasonal menu plus a selection of more than a hundred beers to hundreds of hungry and thirsty patrons seven days a week. And, of course, along the way, also spawning a cookbook.

The pages you hold in your hand constitute our vision of what beer cuisine really means, a vision crafted over not only the five years of beerbistro but also lifetimes of food and beverage exploration. Our goal is to inspire you to try your hand at beer cuisine, as well as introduce you to the food, beer, people, and place that together make up beerbistro. We think it's a pretty great place, and the thousands of diners who have paraded through our doors seem to agree. After making your way through our book, we're hoping you will too.

Cheers!

a little knowledge is a delicious thing

1

Whether in the kitchen or at the table or just kicking back with friends, you're going to get more enjoyment out of your beer if you know a bit about it first. Even on a warm summer day, when all you really want is a thirst-quenching cold one, it helps to know what style of beer is crisper and more refreshing, and which kinds might have too much malty sweetness or aggressive hop bitterness to truly hit the spot.

It is in the kitchen, though, that a little beer-style knowledge really goes a long, long way. Because just as you find very few cookbooks that generically list "meat" or "spice" among the ingredients, so too should you always distrust a recipe that simply calls for "beer." What kind of beer is used—bitter or sweet, light or full-bodied, dry or fruity, potent or mildly alcoholic—will make a major difference in the flavour of the finished dish, so it is essential to know which style is best. It also helps if the cook—that's you!—understands a bit about beer first.

Don't worry—it's not rocket science, just a little Beer 101. And you won't be tested.

Let's start with how beer is made, beginning with what goes into it. Our first ingredient is grain, usually barley, which has been allowed to germinate and then kilned to stop the growth, or, in other words, malted. This not only frees the starches in the barley, which will later be converted into fermentable sugars, then into alcohol, but also toasts the grain to differing degrees of colour, from light gold to deep black. It is these grains, now known as malt, that give the finished beer its hue, so don't be fooled by people who say that dark beer is

About Hops

Originally added to beer as a preservative around 800 CE, hops are the cones of a vine known as *Humulus lupulus* (wolf vine), a member of the same botanical family as *Cannabis sativa*. Typically, hops are added during the boiling portion of the brewing process, much as spices are added to a stew after the base has been made.

Modern brewers use hops primarily for their bittering and aromatic effects. Hops added at the start of the boil will contribute more bitterness, while those added near the end will offer more aroma notes.

The fragrance characteristics of hops range widely from soft florals to strongly nutty or earthy notes and even citrus aromas. Likewise, their bitterness can range from a very light, drying effect to an intensely bitter, sometimes grapefruit-like flavour prized by those die-hard beer aficionados known as "hopheads." Which aromas and flavours come through in the finished beer will depend upon the amount and type of hops used.

"stronger" or more filling than lighter-coloured beer. In the end, it's all about the grain.

The second major ingredient is hops. When we talk about hoppy beers, what we really mean is bitter beers, although in a well-made ale or lager, that bitterness will be balanced by a corresponding amount of malty sweetness.

Third in line is water, which serves as the base or, if you will, the stock for what is essentially a barley and hops stew. Different styles of beer call for water that is either more or less minerally, often because of the makeup of natural resources where the style developed, so, to the brewer, the water used is of immense importance. To those of us who drink and cook with the finished product, however, water is something we can pretty much ignore.

Finally we come to the yeast, which is what takes the sugar-rich, hop-spiced water the brewer crafts and ferments it into beer. Here we come to the two primary families of beer: ale and lager. The older of the two, ales, are fermented by yeast species called *Saccharomyces cerevisiae*, which work at warmer temperatures and gravitate to the top of the fermenter, while the relatively young and now globally popular lagers are fermented by yeasts of the species *S. carlsbergensis*, which function best in cooler temperatures and do their best work at the bottom of the fermenter. We'll look at many substyles in the following pages, but for now remember this: Ales will generally have a fuller body and fruitier palate, while lagers will be crisper, leaner, and more straightforward in taste.

Aside from those almost essential four ingredients (some beers are made without any hops and others without a speck of barley, but these are rare exceptions), brewers can use a whole slew of additional items, from fruits to spices to nuts to chocolate, in creating their beer. Collectively, all these other ingredients are known as adjuncts, and their use, depending on how you look at it, can be either good or bad.

If you ask a German brewer, chances are he will tell you that the only things that belong in beer are barley, hops, yeast, and water, though he will probably stretch to the use of malted wheat, for the wheat beers known as weizens or weissbiers, or malted rye, for an increasingly obscure style of beer called roggen. This attitude is largely due to having learned to make beer under the famed German brewing law, the Reinheitsgebot, which for centuries limited brewers in that country to the four basic ingredients.

Talk to a Belgian or North American brewer, on the other hand, and you'll likely hear a litany of ingredients they think appropriate for brewing. You might be told of beers fermented with whole fruits like raspberries, cherries, and apricots, or be handed a laundry list of herbs and spices and who knows what else! This is because Belgians have always had a bit of a devil-may-care attitude toward brewing, and many young New World brewers have been strongly influenced by the Belgian approach. Also, most of the beers produced in Belgium, Canada, and the United States are ales, which take far more readily to added ingredients than do lagers like the Germans largely produce.

It is, of course, the way in which all these ingredients are put

Beer 101 Cheat Sheet

Malt = sugar, colour (and flavour)

Hops = preservative, bitterness (and flavour)

Yeast = alcohol (and flavour)

Ale = warmer fermentation, fruitier, and rounder body

Lager = cooler fermentation, crisper, and leaner body

The Most Interesting Ingredients We've Found in Beer

Beer flavoured with tobacco? Brewed with carrots and turnips? Spiced with jasmine, freshly ground black pepper, or hibiscus flowers? Yep, we've seen (and tasted) them all, including the following:

- cocoa powder and Madagascar vanilla beans
- seaweed
- smoked jalapeño peppers
- garlic
- wine grapes (cabernet sauvignon, cabernet franc, and merlot)
- peppermint
- spruce boughs
- chicken (really!)

together that makes beers of differing styles. Use pale malt, ample amounts of German hops, and a lager fermentation, and you can make a Pilsner. Add a little darker malt, switch the hops from German to American, and ferment with an ale yeast, and you have an American-style pale ale. Get some black malt in there, cut back on the hops, and ferment it to the point of extreme dryness with an ale yeast, and you have a stout.

The basics, however, remain the same for almost every sort of beer. Once the malt is delivered to the brewhouse, it is coarsely crushed and sent to the mash tun (vat), where warm water is added and the conversion of starches to fermentable sugars begins. After a couple of hours there, what is now called wort (but you can think of it as just flavourful sugar water), is transferred to the brew kettle, where it will be boiled and hops (and possibly other spices) will be added. Once the boil is complete—usually two to three hours—the wort is cooled and sent to the fermenter, where yeast is added and fermentation begins. From there, it's only a matter of time before the beer is ready to drink. (Naturally, this process is much more complicated than this explanation makes it seem, but, hey, that's what we have brewmasters for!)

And Now on to Styles

So we now have beer, but what kind of beer? We know that it's going to be a lager or an ale, depending on what sort of yeast was used to ferment it and at what temperature, but not whether it's going to be sweet or bitter, strong or weak, light or dark. This, naturally enough, is where beer styles come in.

Unlike wine, which can be fairly easily defined by what variety of grape was crushed to make it, beer styles are about broad generalizations. For instance, what one brewery may call an India pale ale, another might deem simply a pale ale, and yet another a golden ale. Frustrating, yes, but arguably no more so than not knowing whether a chardonnay will be a finely nuanced, minerally delight or an oaky bruiser that will have you figuratively picking splinters from between your teeth.

Even so, style guidelines, as imprecise as they may be, do still help sort the wheat from the chaff, so to speak, and, as such, they do matter. All eighty-five of them, if you're to take the number of categories judged at the World Beer Cup, or one hundred or more, if you're to use the rough estimates of some beer authorities. Fortunately, we need not concern ourselves with quite that many styles, since this is, after all, meant as a guiding overview rather than an all-encompassing encyclopedia.

For our purposes, we'll deal with four general categories of beer: Anglo-American ales, Belgian and Belgian-style ales, lagers, and wheat beers.

That's British for "Beer"

Anglo-American ales have their roots in the historic beer styles of the United Kingdom. Principal among these is the style known as pale ale, and its offshoots, India pale ale, or IPA, and double IPA, also known as Imperial pale ale.

Pale ale was born of the need to transport beer long distances, in this case from the brewing town of Burton-on-Trent to the metropolis of London. A slightly elevated alcohol content and increased amount of hops helped preserve the beer through its canal voyage, and a paler malt, new at the time, gave the style its name. The resulting medium-strength beer had a bitter, fruity taste and dry, lingering finish, which, coupled with its lighter hue, made it popular almost instantly. Its cousin, the more bitter, stronger IPA, may have been developed for much the same reason, except that this time the voyage the beer had to take was significantly longer, all the way to the British colonies in India. It was found that the beer actually improved during the voyage!

Double IPA, even stronger at a typical alcohol content of 9 per cent or more, and naturally more bitter, was created in the United States and has nothing to do with the preservative qualities of hops or alcohol. Rather, the most intense style of pale ale was crafted as an extension of the citrusy, more aggressive styles of pale ale and IPA favoured by American craft brewers over the past few decades. So prized is the bite of the hop in some circles, in fact, that devotees of such fiercely bitter brews proudly refer to themselves as "hopheads."

Modern-day black beers also have their roots in England, in this case in a style of ale known then and now as porter. Enjoyed for its balance of roasty malt, coffee-like flavours and hints of chocolate, porter, along with its ebony kin, stout porter—now known simply as stout—was much enjoyed by the busy crews of porters who worked the London docklands in the eighteenth century, and both beers were reputedly named for them.

Over the years, porter all but disappeared, subjugated by the popularity of stout, which of course crossed the sea to Ireland, where it became the very dry, roasty, lightly alcoholic (normally about 4 per cent) brew we know today. Thankfully, though, porter has made a resurgence over the past few decades, along with various substyles of stout, such as the strong, concentrated Imperial stout; the creamy and slightly sweet oatmeal stout, so named for its use of oats along-side malted barley; and various flavoured stouts, including those with added fruits, spices, chocolate, or even the briny liquid from freshly shucked oysters, the last suitably known as oyster stout.

Somewhere between pale ale and stout lies brown ale, a malty, sometimes a bit nutty or minerally style of ale whose roots go back to the dark ales long consumed in British pubs. Its "little brother"—usually a mere 3 to 4 per cent alcohol compared to the brown ale's typical 5 per cent strength—is mild and an even maltier brew that has sadly fallen out of favour with brewers and drinkers alike over the past few decades.

Also on the malty-chocolaty-toffee-ish side of the flavour ledger are the ale styles of Scotland, normally called simply Scottish ales but sometimes referred to by their historical designation of 70, 80, or 90 shilling beers, which refers to an old method of taxing beer based on strength. The strongest of these, sometimes called wee heavies or, more commonly, Scotch ales, can reach alcohol contents of 8 per cent or more, and tend to have treacly, almost molasses-like textures and tastes.

Finally, at the strong end of the Anglo-American scale, we have barleywine, spelled as one word or two, or, to comply with various labelling laws, sometimes called barleywine-style ale. In keeping with British style, it is very malty, very strong, and typically sweet and fruity, somewhat reminiscent of port wine in character. Its U.S. version is extremely hoppy and very strong, with flavour and aroma notes approximating dried fruit, tanned leather, and complex spice. In both styles, this is a beer that may be cellar aged, in some cases for up to several decades.

Eccentric, Enticing Belgium

Moving along to Belgian and Belgian-style ales, things get both simpler and more confusing. From a cooking perspective, Belgian ales are relatively easy to understand because they almost universally tend toward a sweet and malty profile, with some notable exceptions, of course. Confusion arises, however, because of the eccentricities exhibited by many if not most Belgian brewers. Ask what style of beer they make, and chances are the reply you'll receive is a plain "My style."

Still, some rough styles do exist, beginning with the oft-employed descriptor abbey ale.

The roots of the abbey or abbey-style ale are found in the beers produced by Belgium's six Trappist monastery breweries. ("Trappist" is a designation legally protected by the brothers, which is why the more generic "abbey" is commonly used.) Typically, although not necessarily, these beers are strong, malty, and sweet, often with spicy notes that arise from fermentation rather than any addition of spice, or mild to profound chocolaty flavours. Often they will be referred to by the Flemish name dubbel, which harkens back to when the abbeys brewed in two strengths, a weaker ale, known as enkel, or single, for daily drinking and a more robust dubbel for feast days. (Some enkels are still brewed commercially, although rarely so. When seen, they are often blonde in colour, with a fruity-malty-spicy flavour and 4 to 5 per cent alcohol content.)

Another abbey-rooted style is triple, or tripel, which references the strong, golden, dryly spicy ale of the Trappist abbey at Westmalle. This beer, developed only after World War II for commercial purposes, gave rise near the end of the twentieth century to an even stronger, darkly malty, and more intense style called quadrupel. It should be noted that none of these numerical designations is meant to imply a multiplication of strength, but merely a gradual rise in potency.

Among the most challenging of Belgian beer styles are the sour ales of the Flemish north, frequently divided into red and brown categories. These moderately strong, fruity beers, which derive their characteristic tartness from the influence of various micro-organisms during fermentation, most importantly a "bug" called *Brettanomyces*, remain somewhat obscure in their home country today but have found a strong following among beer aficionados in North America and elsewhere. Because of their unusual character, which can tend

The Trappists

Of all the world's monastic breweries, and there are many, only an exclusive and much revered seven bear the label Trappist, six of which are located in Belgium and one in the Netherlands. Although better known by the names of their beers, each abbey has a lengthy, official name:

- Sint Benedictusabdij de Achelse Kluis (Achel)
- Abbaye Notre-Dame de Scourmont (Chimay)
- Abbaye Notre-Dame d'Orval (Orval)
- Abbaye Notre-Dame de Saint-Rémy (Rochefort)
- Abdij der Trappisten van Westmalle (Westmalle)
- Sint Sixtus Trappistenbdij (Westvleteren)
- Konigshoeven Abdij (La Trappe or, in some jurisdictions, Konigshoeven)

Of these seven, only the rare ales of Westvleteren are not represented at beerbistro.

Running the Right Temperature

If you're like most people, you keep your beer in the fridge. But did you know that for optimum flavour and aroma, certain beer styles should be served at different temperatures? So the next time you're pouring a beer for yourself or your guests, try to match as closely as possible the following temperatures:

Refrigerator temperature (about 3°C/35-37°F)

- most lagers (Pilsner, dunkel, helles, Vienna lager)
- most wheats (Belgian, German, lambic, fruit beers)
- lighter ales (cream ales, Kölsch)

Warmed up slightly out of the fridge (about 6-7°C/45°F)

- most ales of moderate strength (pale ale, best bitter, IPA, brown ale)
- strong lagers (bock, doppelbock, Märzen)

even toward vinegary in some extreme cases, they are exceptionally useful in the kitchen.

Another style for which the Belgians are known is *saison*, from the French word for "season." These blonde ales are among the hoppiest of the traditional Belgian brews, as they were originally brewed in the spring for storage and consumption over the long, non-brewing summer months. (In the past, before the modernization of brewing and isolation of yeast strains, the plethora of airborne bacteria in the summertime made fermentation at best an uncertain proposition.) Dry, mildly to moderately bitter, ofttimes spicy, and slightly strong at about 6 to 7 per cent alcohol, these ales are fine thirst quenchers despite their relative potency.

Flavoured ales, whose tastes are influenced by a wide variety of assorted ingredients, from fruit to spices and herbs, are often thought of as a specifically Belgian style, even though their roots go back thousands of years to the earliest days of brewing. What *is* true, however, is that the Belgian influence is likely the cause for the resurgence in popularity these beers have experienced over the past couple of decades. Since they come in any number of varieties, strengths, and intensities, these brews, as well as the myriad other singular beers produced in Belgium or sold under the rubric of "Belgian-style," are best dealt with on a case-by-case basis.

Lager: Conquering the Brewing World

The word "lager" stems from the German word *lagern*, which means "to store in a cool place." Its use reflects the roots of lager fermentation, which was discovered by accident about one thousand years ago when Bavarian brewers began storing their beers in ice caves situated at the foot of the Alps, thus providing the ideal environment for a new kind of yeast to get involved in fermentation. (For the seven or so thousand years of brewing history prior, all beer was ale.) Drinkers liked the new taste—even if brewers, not at that time understanding the workings of yeast, had only the faintest idea of what was going on—and the new beer caught on.

Centuries later, in 1842, a Bavarian brewer brought his talents to a town in what is now the Czech Republic and combined lager fermentation with a newly available pale gold malt and an indigenous variety of hops known as Saaz. The town was Pilsen, and the beer, the first golden lager ever brewed, was named Pilsner.

Today, all the world's most popular beers find their roots in that Pilsner, whether they're brewed in the Netherlands, Japan, or the United States. But those aren't the beers you're going to find put to much use in the following pages. Rather, the varieties of Pilsner we'll be more concerned with are Bohemian, German, and Continental.

While these three beer styles appear similar—golden, with a white, frothy head—their aromas and tastes differ considerably. The original Bohemian style has a moderate bitterness at least partially offset by a caramelly or even slightly butterscotchy maltiness and a fragrant, floral aroma. The German style, on the other hand, is drier and more apparently hoppy, with a restrained, even thin maltiness. The Continental version is a sweeter beer, with a light bitterness, balanced malt, and little to none of the caramel notes found in its Czech parent brew.

Temperature, cont'd

Cellar temperature (about 10–12°C/50–55°F)

- strong ales (barleywine, Imperial or double IPA, dubbel)
- black ales (stout, porter, Imperial stout)

As a rule of thumb, the darker and stronger a beer is, the warmer it should be served. (Notable exceptions to this guideline are tripel and other strong, blonde ales of Belgian origin, which should always be served cold.) To hit your temperatures without having three differently cooled refrigerators, just plan your beers a bit in advance, taking the cellar-temperature ones out of the fridge about an hour before serving them and the middle-tier ones out about 30 minutes prior to service.

Next to Pilsner—and its various offshoots, including most globally mass-marketed brands—all other styles of lager are pretty small-time. Likely the next best known is bock, which is named after either the German word for "billy goat" or a corruption of the name of the town of Einbeck, depending on which story you believe. (The more plausible one is the latter, given that it seems likely this sort of beer was first brewed in that northern German city.) It is malty and mild to moderately sweet—yet still possesses a lager's characteristic crispness—and generally dark of hue, with an above-average strength of about 6 to 7 per cent alcohol. Its principal off-shoot is the doppelbock, or "double bock," an even maltier, sweeter, and stronger brew with monastic origins similar to those of the abbey ale known as dubbel.

Other styles of lager rooted in Germany include the pale Bavarian lager called helles, from the German for "light," which is stylistically similar to a Continental Pilsner except with a greater maltiness and relatively mild bitterness, and its darker, toasty, earthy kin, dunkel. The stronger, sweeter, golden beer often associated with Oktoberfest and known as Märzen—pronounced "mare-tzen"—can be thought of as a bigger version of the helles.

Completing the lager family is one from Austria and another from the former East Germany, plus an anomaly from the part of eastern Bavaria called Franconia. The first is aptly named Vienna lager and is generally rich gold to light amber in colour and lightly sweet at the beginning but dry and a bit toasty in the finish, while the East German brew is a black lager known as schwarzbier.

Although its dark hue often fools people into believing it to be rich and filling, schwarzbier is typically a mild-mannered brew, moderately strong, with a light body and low bitterness.

Probably the world's most unusual lager is the style known as rauchbier, or "smoked beer." Strongly linked to the town of Bamberg, Germany, rauchbier is well named, as it is typically crafted from barley malt that has been first smoked over a wooden fire, giving the finished beer a smokiness that some have likened to "smoked ham in a glass" or, less charitably, an ashtray. Definitely a love-it-or-hate-it style, its aficionados—among whom we number ourselves—hail it as a taste experience like no other.

Finally, Wheat

Certainly the most common misconception about wheat beers is that they are brewed entirely from wheat. They are not. While some German wheat beers employ up to 80 per cent malted wheat, most use considerably less, and the Belgian style contains as little as 35 per cent, with the balance in both cases being composed of malted barley. But we're getting ahead of ourselves.

German-style wheat beers are light, refreshing, and slightly citrusy. Variously known as weizen (wheat), hefeweizen (wheat with yeast), or weissbier (white beer), any of these three forms are likely to have yeast in the bottle (only a label that reads "kristal" will guarantee a filtered beer). They have undergone a fermentation that yields flavour and aroma notes of clove and banana, both of which are characteristic of the family of ale yeasts usually used to ferment these beers and have nothing to do with spice or fruit additions. A much stronger, darker, and spicier version of a weissbier, sometimes called weizenbock, is also produced by some breweries.

Given what you already know about Belgian beers, you've likely already guessed that their version of wheat beer—variously known as bière blanche or wit, both of which mean "white beer"—has added spices, specifically coriander and bitter orange peel. (Some brewers may add to this spice bill, but all true Belgian or Belgian-style wits will contain those two spices.) Additionally, unmalted wheat will be used in addition to barley malt, which gives this spicy, fruity brew an even lighter character than that of its German counterpart.

A second variety of Belgian wheat beer is something called lambic, which is the only spontaneously fermented style of beer commercially brewed today. That means that traditional lambics are fermented by wild, airborne yeasts, then conditioned in wooden barrels for a year or more before being blended with other lambics to form the champagne-esque beer called gueuze, or refermented with fruit to make kriek (cherry beer), framboise (raspberry), or a host of other fruit beers.

The problem with lambic arises in its commercialization, since while traditional examples will be bone-dry, often tart, and remarkably complex, more heavily produced and marketed versions can bear more resemblance to alcohol "coolers" than to beer. As with so many beer styles and brands out there, the key to finding out which is which lies in asking the person selling the beer—and, of course, plenty of experience.

Beer Tasting 101

When we host beer tastings at the restaurant, one of the most common questions we field is, "What's the right way to taste beer?" The answer is, "Any way!" So long as you're sipping and appreciating the beer, it's pretty much guaranteed that you're doing it the right way.

For professional tasters, of course, the process is a little different. So if you're an aspiring beer reviewer, or simply want to be able to lead your friends in a proper tasting, here are some general steps to follow. As you read through them, you'll quickly realize that it's not much different from tasting wine, except for the fact that beer tasters never, ever spit!

Step 1: Admire the beer. This might seem kind of silly, but brewers go to great lengths to get just the right colour to their beer, so it's only right that we take some time to appreciate it. Besides, if you look closely, the beer could be telling you something. If it has been properly poured and yet has little to no foam, for instance, it could be that the beer is a little old. If the colour has developed a brassy tinge, it could mean that the beer has oxidized. And if it's hazy when there is no yeast present in the bottle, well, that might just signal some problems at the brewery or on the bottling line.

Step 2: Smell the beer. This might draw you some odd looks at the bar (except at beerbistro, of course!), but appreciating the aroma is essential to getting the most out of any beer. If you're skeptical, try this test. First, sip the beer from a clean glass and note all the flavours you can taste. Then try it again, but with your nose plugged. With your sense of smell cut off, the beer is sure to taste a lot plainer than when you tried it the first time.

If you're tasting an ale, try to detect fruity aromas, whereas if it's a lager, look for notes of straw, hay, fresh-cut grass, or, if it's a malty lager like a bock, hints of toffee or caramel. If it's a hoppy ale, be prepared for aromas from nuttiness to spice to lemon or grapefruit zest.

Step 3: Taste the beer. This is what you've been waiting for, right? So take your time with it. Sip slowly, allowing the beer to roll over your tongue and around the sides of your mouth, and appreciate the flavours before you swallow. Then think about the taste. Is it bitter? Spicy? Nutty? Does the flavour linger on your tongue? Now try another taste, only this time, after you sip, purse your lips and take in a little air. This will aerate the beer in your mouth and bring out the flavours more strongly.

Again, ales have fruitier flavours, and lagers will be leaner and crisper on the palate. Malty beers will have richer flavours, from stewed plum to coffee, candied nuts, and chocolate, while hoppier beers will have bitter tastes like citrus peel, green roots, nutshell, and brown spice.

Step 4: Swallow and consider. Aftertaste is important in beer, which is why we swallow while those wine people keep spitting. So after you taste, consider what you've tasted and what flavours remain on your palate. The flavours should flow naturally, without any abrupt changes from, say, sweet to bitter or fruity to nutty, and stretch out languorously on your palate, fading slowly from your taste buds.

Writing down what you're just experienced is a good way to get to know both beer and your own palate, but often it's more than enough to just appreciate, enjoy, and move on to the next taste.

2

beer at the table

When company is coming, the table has been set with the good silver, and something special is on the menu, nine times out of ten—perhaps ninety-nine times out of one hundred—corks are poised to be popped. Depending on what food is to be served, the beverage of choice might be chardonnay, cabernet, or pinot noir, but chances are high it will be some sort of wine.

Ever wonder why that is?

Steeped as we are in the romance of the grape, most of us do it automatically, not even considering that there might be better gastronomic matches for our prize roast or trademark seafood stew. We do it because our parents did it, and they did it, quite frankly, because the French did it. And what we learned in the early years of advanced gastronomy in the West we learned largely from the French.

But what if we had taken our early culinary cues from the Belgians instead? After all, they arguably eat better than their European neighbours do, a notion espoused by even the legendary French chef Paul Bocuse, who once described Belgian cuisine as "French food improved." And as opposed to wine-swilling Parisians, the citizens of Brussels, Antwerp, and Liège are far more open-minded in their choice of mealtime beverage, opting at times for wine, yes, but equally or even more often choosing beer.

Given the range of styles and flavours found in the Belgian beer-scape, this is hardly surprising. Indeed, when you stop to consider the assortment of tastes to be found in the wide world's ales and lagers, from sweet chocolate and cherries to dry bitterness and vibrant spice, it only makes sense to dine with beer. Its lower average alcohol content makes it easy to try different styles with different courses, its extraordinary range of tastes makes pairing with even the most wine-unfriendly foods a breeze, and, of course, the affordability of beer takes a lot of pressure off the wallet. Truly, beer is the natural partner to almost any cuisine.

The only question is where to begin.

At beerbistro, every dish on the menu comes with a suggested beer companion, as do most recipes in this book, but there's no reason that your dining-with-beer experiences should end there. Especially when, using a few basic guidelines and a bit of common sense, crafting delectable food and beer partnerships is as easy as pouring a pint of stout.

How to Pour a Beer

Seems pretty simple, doesn't it? Pop the cap, grab a glass, pour, drink. Basic stuff.

Except that it's not really that easy. There's foaming to consider, not enough of which can be as bad as too much, and the possibility of yeast in the bottle. Fact is, with the proliferation of beer styles today, you need a few tips if you're going to get the most out of your beer.

Pour #1: A Basic Beer

This standard beer pour works for most basic beer styles, from Pilsner to pale ale, and when executed correctly will yield a delicious-looking glass of ale or lager.

1. Pick a glass. A choice beer glass will be reserved for beer and beer alone, and washed with hot water only. Detergents and soap residues cling to the inside of the glass and are sure foam killers.

2. Start the pour. The angle at which you hold the glass will determine the amount of foam that forms—the closer you hold it to horizontal, the less foam you'll get—so start at about a 45° angle and let the foam build naturally.

3. Continue the pour. At about the halfway point, you should have an idea of how the head is building. You're aiming for about 3 to 4 cm (1 to 1½ inches) of foam, so flatten out the angle of the glass if too much foam is showing or straighten it up if there's not enough. (A good "collar" of foam not only releases all the aromas in the beer but also looks great!)

4. Get ready to drink. Finish the pour with the glass just about vertical, allowing a bit of room for the last bubbles to rise to the top and create an extra 0.5 cm (¼ inch) or so of head after you've stopped pouring. Cheers!

Pour #2: A Hefeweizen (German Wheat Beer)

This German style of wheat beer has a pour all its own, since part of the flavour component is the yeast that sits at the bottom of the bottle. (When yeast is present in the bottle, it means the beer has undergone a final bottle fermentation or has been bottled unfiltered.) If you wish to skip step 2, gently roll the bottle on a flat surface prior to opening and pouring it. Whenever possible, use a classic hefeweizen glass for these beers.

1. Start the pour. Because of the bottle fermentation, hefeweizens generate a lot of head when poured, so start the pour with the glass on a very steep angle, as close to horizontal as you can get.

2. Capture the yeast. At about the three-quarters point of the pour, with a good 4 to 5 cm (about 2 inches) of foam already formed, stop. Hold the bottle by the neck and gently twirl it a few times to stir up whatever yeast may be stuck to the bottom.

3. Finish with a flourish. Holding the glass vertically, pour the remaining beer and yeast into the middle of the existing foam. Now you should have a cloud of foam atop your beer, stretching above the lip of the glass, with a slight darkness from the yeast in the centre.

Pour #3: An Abbey Ale (and Most Other Bottle-Fermented Ales)

Many strong ales, from Trappist ales to barleywines to Imperial stouts, undergo a final bottle fermentation and so are bottled with active yeast. Unlike hefeweizens, however, this yeast is generally not intended for consumption in the beer, since its addition will change the taste of the ale. (Not that this yeast is bad, mind you, since it is actually jam-packed with vitamins. We suggest drinking it separately as a sort of brewer's multivitamin.) So with ales of this sort, you want to decant the beer and leave the sediment behind.

1. Start the pour. Depending on the beer, bottle-fermented ales may foam aggressively or need coaxing to work up a proper head, so start this pour cautiously and react by increasing or decreasing the angle of the glass as needed.

2. Keep pouring. Pour quickly or slowly, but just keep pouring! If you stop and restart, the yeast may get stirred up and mixed into the beer.

3. Finish up. When you see the level in the bottle drop to about 1 cm (½ inch), stop the pour. What's left is nutritious brewer's yeast, plus a little beer. It's perfectly acceptable to drink your "multivitamin" straight out of the bottle before you begin enjoying your beer.

Beaumont's Four Steps to Pairing Beer and Food

1: Think of Ale as Red Wine and Lager as White Wine

Since most people are familiar with the rudimentaries of partnering wine with food, we've found it helps to use this knowledge as a starting point for learning about the harmonies to be found between beer and food. So if you're inclined to follow prevailing wisdom and serve a full-bodied red alongside a steak, for instance, you can choose an equally robust ale, such as, say, a Belgian-style dubbel, to serve the same purpose. Or if you'd prefer a delicate, aromatic white with a piece of sole sautéed in lemon and parsley, choose a helles as a beer option.

The parallels continue. As with red wines, ales are more likely to pair well with winter stews, while white wines and lagers are better suited to lighter, warm-weather fare like a picnic spread of sandwiches and potato salad. And just as some lighter reds can complement dishes you'd ordinarily pair with a white wine, so are some of the less heavy-handed styles of ale harmonious with a wide range of foods, including some you'd expect would be more lager-friendly.

Where this guideline runs into trouble is with wheat beers, which while being technically ales actually act more like lagers at the table. (Belgian wits and German hefeweizens in particular are excellent with salads and egg dishes.) As well, because beer is so versatile at the table, some foods you would never dream of pairing with a white wine, such as a thick hamburger fresh off the barbecue, can be deliciously accompanied by a fairly hoppy Pilsner, largely due to the dynamics explained in step 2.

2: Hoppiness in Beer = Acidity in Wine

A less recognized guideline for pairing wine with food has it that the more spice or fat or salt you have in a dish, the more acidity you will want in the wine. This works for beer too, except that instead of acidity, here we look for hoppiness.

This is an easy one to try for yourself. Start with two beers, one fairly hoppy and bitter, such as a pale ale, and the other malty and perhaps a bit sweet, like a Scotch ale. Next, grab a bag of salty snacks—potato chips or pretzels will do—and try them first with the hoppy beer and then alongside the malty one.

What you should find is that the salt on the snack will sour the maltiness of the Scotch ale and make it taste, well, sort of flat and cardboard-like, while the vibrant hoppiness of the pale ale will strip away the lingering salt, refresh the palate, and not only allow you to better enjoy the freshness of the beer but also make the next pretzel or potato chip taste that much better. This effect is accentuated further when there is more fat involved, as with French fries, for instance, since the oils in the food will pretty much glue the salt to your palate and make it difficult to taste anything—until, that is, the fresh hoppiness of a German Pilsner or American pale ale arrives to cut the salty fat and revive your taste buds.

When we note this concept with regard to spicy food, many people counter with the common pairing of Mexican or Indian lagers with their respective fiery cuisines. But most of the time when such light lagers are presented alongside a burrito or curry, they're served ice cold, which means that the beer is anesthetizing the palate rather than harmonizing with the peppery flavours. Try a chilled—but not frozen—hoppy beer instead and you'll find that the bitterness will calm the heat while still allowing the taste of the peppers, and all the other ingredients, to shine through.

3: Complement or Contrast

Now we get to the heart of the matter—flavour! In an axiom that is as true for beer as it is for wine or any other beverage, when seeking to pair food and drink, look for flavour profiles that either complement or contrast each other. (Many cooks and food and beverage writers will include a third C—cut—but we find that cutting one flavour with another, as when you slice through the richness of a cream sauce with a hoppy Pilsner, is much the same as building a contrasting relationship.) Do this and you'll be well on your way to creating a most tasteful and dynamic menu.

Of the two, complementary relationships are the easiest to forge. Start with the dish you're seeking to pair and examine it for flavour notes that might find parallels in beer. Is it resinous with rosemary or thyme? Pick a beer with herbaceous or "grassy" hop notes. Does it have a rich, full, complex character? Look for a similar ale. Is it fragrant with saffron or ginger? Reach for a suitably aromatic spiced beer. And so on and so on.

Contrasting relationships are the tougher ones, since they are seldom straightforward. On the plus side, however, they can also be immensely rewarding simply because they are so unexpected.

When pulling together marriages of contrasting parts, be sure to first identify a flavour trigger that pulls the disparate tastes together. For instance, the roasted malt normally used in the making of a dry stout often gives the beer a faintly salty taste. This establishes a common ground of sorts for the partnership of stout and briny oysters, even though the full and roasty flavour of the black ale would seem at odds with the delicacy of a freshly shucked bivalve. Similarly, the soft buttery taste of a Bohemian Pilsner provides the link between that beer and a rich and creamy fettuccine Alfredo, even though the lager and pasta would seem to be polar opposites in taste.

One final note on complements and contrasts: don't be shy or afraid to experiment! At a beer and food festival, we once tasted a most exceptional and entirely illogical pairing that put together a citrus-filled chocolate truffle and a German-style Pilsner. Rationally speaking, and according to all our experience, it shouldn't have worked, and yet there it was, a beer and food marriage that was even more delicious than the sum of its individually quite tasty parts—and a reminder that sometimes even the best rules are made for breaking.

4: Keep the Beer Sweeter than the Dessert

We don't dislike wine and in fact enjoy it often, both on its own and with a meal. But we also believe strongly that beer is the more versatile beverage at the table, and at no time is this more evident than when dessert is served.

Ask a typical sommelier to recommend a beverage partner for your chocolate cake, crème brulée, or fruit tart and he or she will usually fumble around a bit before suggesting something that's almost but not quite a suitable match. Make the same request of someone schooled in beer, however, and you will be rewarded with an abundance of choice, from strong and malty barleywine (for the cake) to spicy blonde Belgian ale (for the crème brulée), and boldly flavourful fruit beer (for the tart). Beer is a natural fit for all these post-prandial pleasures, and many, many more besides, so long as you keep one thought in mind—sweetness.

With a single, most notable exception—more about that in a bit—it is very important when pairing beer and desserts that the beer stay sweeter than the dish. This way, the voyage back and forth between ale and cake or bock and pudding will be seamless and most enjoyable. If the dessert is more sugary than the beer, however, your strong spiced ale or doppelbock will wind up tasting sour, which will in turn reflect badly on the next forkful of the dish and so on, right into a downward spiral of offensive tastes.

The notable exception to this guideline is chocolate, which actually has much in common with beer. Only the most informed chocoholics are aware of the fact that cacao beans must ferment before chocolate can be produced from them, just like beer, and the taste of that finished chocolate is not sweet but bitter, just like hops. With these two flavour traits in common, the way is clear for beer and chocolate to become fast friends, which they most certainly do, whether in a cake or pudding or while consumed together. At beerbistro, we even make some very popular chocolate ice creams with beer! (And so will you too, once you read the recipes for them on pages 229 and 230.)

Now Get Started!

These four basic steps to food and beer happiness are just a starting point. Now the experimentation must begin!

It would be grand if it were possible to prescribe some hard and fast rules for food and beverage pairing but, alas, the gastronomic world simply doesn't work that way. For every rule or step, there exists a multitude of exceptions—like the truffle and Pilsner partnership that shouldn't have worked but did—and so, in the end, the best teacher is and always will be experience.

In math and science, there are constants; at the table, there are not. Your palate will be different from ours, and the flavours that make sense in your mouth won't necessarily be those that express themselves best to your friends or relatives. With spice, for instance, some people much prefer the soothing contrast of sweetness to the hoppy bite of bitterness, and who are we to disagree?

That's the beauty of taste: no one is right and no one is wrong.

So beginning with some of our recipes, or even with a few bottles of beer and a couple of different kinds of cheese or chocolate or cold cuts, start experimenting to find how you most enjoy the combination of beer and food. Because, as we always tell people at beerbistro, the only sure way to know what's right for you is to practise, practise, practise.

Seven Steps to Hosting a Home Beer Tasting

1. Get a plan. Sure you can have a bunch of friends come over to sample random beers, but it will be more fun (and even educational) if you choose a theme to follow. This could be a country, a style (or two or three), or even beers well suited to a specific season. Examples include Belgian beers, stouts and porters, winter warmers (high-alcohol beers, but keep the tasting portions small!), or the beers of summer (Pilsners, light ales, and wheat beers).

2. Get your beers. Choose the beers you want to taste carefully, selecting a mix of brands people might know and others that few will have even heard of. Eight to ten different beers is a good number, allowing for about 100 mL (3½ ounces) of each per person.

3. Get your equipment. People need something to drink from, right? So tasting glassware is a must—wine glasses work well—but there's more to equipping a tasting than just that. You'll need water pitchers and water glasses so that people can cleanse their palate, stay hydrated, and rinse their glasses (so you need provide only one per person!), plus some bread or unsalted crackers for those who prefer to freshen their taste buds that way. Also, keep some dump buckets handy so that no one feels obliged to finish everything in their glass—spare pitchers and ice buckets are terrific for this.

4. Get rid of stuff. You don't want flowers, scented candles, or a burning barbeque around, since strong smells will prevent your guests from properly tasting the beers. Also not required are tasting sheets, since those do nothing more than intimidate novice beer tasters. (You can keep a few sheets of paper handy for those who will want to make notes.)

5. Get informed. As host, your guests are going to look to you when they have questions about certain beers, so it's best if you know how to answer them. No need to become a walking beer encyclopedia—just get to know the basics of the beers you're serving. Perhaps keep this cookbook handy for quick reference.

6. Get started. Again, your duties as host beckon. When your guests arrive, offer them a warm-up beer first, something not too hoppy or strong and in modest quantity, to get the palate ready for tasting. Then explain what is available to sample and suggest an order to taste them in, starting lighter and weaker and heading toward the fuller-bodied, stronger beers.

7. Get done. When the tasting fun is over, people are going to want to kick back with a beer and socialize. So at this stage, you'll want to have some food at the ready, and larger glasses too, so that people who want a full beer can pour it all at once. (Don't forget to plan for this when buying your beer.)

3

beer in the kitchen

Naturally, the idea behind this book is to bring beer into your kitchen and get you cooking the recipes. But we also believe that every cookbook should be the beginning of a journey, rather than a destination in and of itself, so to start you on your own voyage into beer cuisine, we've gathered together a few hints and tips from years of research and experience in the beerbistro kitchen. Use them wisely and get cooking!

Marinate It!

One of the most popular ways to use beer in the kitchen for both amateur and professional cooks, marinating provides not only flavour but also tenderness and moisture to everything from beef to chicken and fish. The trick is simply to choose the right beer for the job.

Ideally, the intensity of flavour in the ingredient being marinated should match that of the beer. Rather than marinating beef in light lager, for example, you'll want a more robust beer style, such as brown ale or porter, while for more delicate proteins like chicken and whitefish, you'll want beers with gentler tastes, such as wheat beers, pale lagers, and fruit beers. The beerbistro kitchen is particularly jazzed about using fruit beers with chicken for the sweetish, fruity appeal they bestow.

Another quality to watch in the beer is hoppiness, since the kind of long, slow cooking often associated with marinated foods will intensify the bitterness of an IPA or Imperial stout.

Timing Cures and Marinations

Marinate

Fish 15–30 minutes, to a maximum of 1 hour

Pork 4–16 hours (or overnight)

Beef 18 hours–2 days

Cure

Fish 12–36 hours

Pork 4–7 days

Foie gras 2 days

Duck 7 days

Cure It!

When curing meats and fish, try to find beers with flavour characteristics normally associated with the particular food being cured. If you want to cure a ham, for instance, a hefeweizen makes a good choice because of its clove and fruit flavours.

When curing ingredients with beer, people can often become overly concerned with colour, since there's the fear that a dark beer will discolour the food. Our advice: Forget about it! Sure there may be some colour added to the outside of the meat, poultry, or fish, but once it's cut or carved, the natural hue of whatever has been cured will still persist.

Dress It!

Beer, and especially fruit beers, can be a great addition to vinaigrettes and salad dressings. If a traditional lambic is used, one that is tart and assertive, then it can be used as a good substitute for vinegar, while fruitier beers, like some brown ales and of course all fruit beers, can add great depths of taste to dressings for salads of all sorts. Belgian and Belgian-style wheat beers are also wonderful in vinaigrettes, since they add both spiciness and fruitiness. Just remember when using non-traditional lambics to always balance out the beer with vinegar or citrus juice so the desired acidity of the dressing is maintained.

Grill It!

There's a fondness in some quarters for basting meats with beer while they're grilling, but we think this is just a waste of good beer. Since the alcohol content in beer is usually too low to cause flaring, you won't get any caramelization of residual sugars the way you would when basting with, say, bourbon, and the high water content of the beer that sprays over the fire is just going to lower your cooking temperature or create unwanted spots of coolness in the fire.

One way the beerbistro kitchen has found to use beer on the grill is by adding bread crumbs and malty Belgian ale to the ground lamb mixture in our burgers (recipe, page 159). Since the bread will catch and absorb the beer, the ale's sugars are left in the meat to caramelize on the grill, thus producing more flavour and a tasty crust around the outside of the meat. You can apply this technique to any kind of burger, from pork to fish, so long as you avoid hoppy beers, and the beer's character matches that of the meat.

Poach It!

When poaching food in beer, stay away from hoppy beers—the heat will make the hop oils exceptionally volatile and create a very bitter taste. In the extreme, hoppy beers can actually tear apart poached seafood, leaving you with a mess rather than a meal.

Sauté It!

Use beer sparingly when sautéing, since what you're after is a dry rather than wet heat. One way to bring the taste of beer to your stir-fries, though, is by cooking the base rice in a light Pilsner, light ale, or fruit beer. Avoid hoppy brews, as they produce bitter rice.

Steam It!

For the most part, steam is steam is steam, so don't waste your beer by using it to steam vegetables. If steaming meat over beer, however, or using beer to steam rice, remember to match flavour characteristics so that the taste of the beer doesn't overwhelm the flavour of what's being steamed and, again, be careful with hoppiness.

Sauce It!

When creating a sauce, you may be tempted to add a little beer directly to the pot. Don't! Instead, try reducing the beer first to intensify its character, then add it slowly to your sauce, tasting all the way so you don't overwhelm the other flavours. Naturally, malty beers work best for this application.

Hoppy beers, on the other hand, can add great taste to spicy sauces like curries and piquant pasta sauces, but these need not be reduced first, since their bitterness may then become too intensified. Do make sure you add the beer when the sauce is very hot, although not boiling, so as to reduce the alcohol content while maintaining the taste and balance.

Finally, tread cautiously when adding dark beers to light-coloured sauces, since nobody wants, say, a brown cream sauce.

Stew It!

There's hardly been a stew invented that can't get a bit of a flavour boost from beer, so long as the ale or lager selected has a character that reflects that of the stew. For a robust lamb stew, try a full and malty beer, such as a Scotch ale or sweet porter, while a light chicken or vegetarian stew would benefit more from a cream ale or pale lager.

Hoppiness is of less concern when picking a beer for a stew because of the long, slow cooking times. Since hop oils grow volatile only when the boiling point is reached, if you keep the stew on simmer,

pale ales or even IPAS can be used to add flavour and character. Remember that hoppy ales tend to fuse better with spicy flavours or, alternately, resinous herbal flavours like rosemary and fresh thyme.

Batter It!

When used in a batter for deep-frying, beer adds great delicacy by strengthening the bonds in the flour and adding airiness through its carbonation. Just watch carefully the colour and hoppiness of the beer used, since nobody wants a batter that's too dark or too bitter.

Bake It!

"Beer is liquid bread," says Brian, so it's only natural to use beer in making everything from sandwich loaves to baguettes to hamburger buns. What's more, because bread is more savoury than, say, cake or pie crust, there's room to use some hoppy beers, thus adding a faint but appealing bitter edge to the dough.

Where dessert baking is concerned, Brian says, "Never in my life have I baked a cake with hoppy beer." So we suggest staying away from Pilsners, pale ales, and IPAS.

A lot of the time, baking with beer is simply a matter of substituting the water, milk, or cream in the recipe with a suitable beer. Remember that if anything fatty is being replaced, such as milk or cream, you'll need to add some butter to make up for the lost fat.

One bonus of using beer in cake and other sweet batters is that, because of the carbonation, the end product will be even lighter and fluffier than if it were prepared without beer.

Sweeten It!

When using beers in desserts, always pick a style with an assertive character or the taste of the beer will be lost to the sugar content of the dish. Stronger beers, such as Belgian and Belgian-style spiced ales and old malty ales, work best in this regard, since they'll have not only full flavours but also a good amount of residual sugar. Hoppy beers don't work well because they add bitterness.

Fruit beers work beautifully in whipped dishes like zabaglione and with poached fruit like pears and apples. Strong, abbey-style ales and chocolate are also natural partners, both in the oven and at the table.

Beer Styles à la beerbistro

By now, you're no doubt a pro when it comes to beer styles, but not everyone is so advanced. This is why we developed our own unique way of classifying beers at beerbistro, one that speaks more to the experience the beer delivers than it does to a style or a nation of origin.

Listed below with brief explanations are our basic beer categories. Throughout the recipes that follow, you will find one or more of these categories of beer recommended as an accompaniment to the recipes or, in many cases, as a descriptor of the beer called for in the recipe. As you work through the book, these will become increasingly familiar and act as a sort of shorthand for more traditional beer styles, but to start you off, here is a quick overview of the categories and their meanings.

Quenching—Softly spicy and fruity German- and Belgian-style wheat beers. Look for hefeweizens, such as Hacker-Pschorr Weiss and Schneider Weiss; or Belgian and Belgian-style wheat beers, such as Blanche de Chambly, Blue Moon, and Hoegaarden.

Crisp—Dry and refreshing lagers ranging from moderately bitter to robustly hoppy. Look for Czech and Czech-style lagers, such as Pilsner Urquell and King Pilsner; German and German-style pilsners, such as Bitburger Pils and Victory Prima Pils; or hoppy pale or golden lagers, such as Brooklyn Lager.

Appetizing—Ales endowed with subtle shades of tartness, fruitiness, and mouth-wateringly dry malt. Look for any of a wide range of such international beers, from Rodenbach Grand Cru to traditional lambics, such as Cantillon Gueuze, to New World, barrel-aged beers, such as New Belgium La Folie and Panil Barriqué.

Sociable—Ales and lagers with moderate strength, medium body, and near-perfect balance. Look for less hoppy beers, such as De Koninck and Cameron's Auburn Ale; unique products, such as Cooper's Sparkling Ale and Anchor Steam Beer; and light bitters, such as Big Rock Traditional Ale.

Satisfying—Ales, porters, and stouts with gentle bitterness and chocolaty or roasty character. Look for British and Irish stouts and porters, such as O'Hara's Celtic Stout and Fuller's London Porter; Old World–inspired black beers, such as St. Ambroise Oatmeal Stout; and brown ales, such as Hobgoblin Ale and Black Oak Nut Brown Ale.

Bold—Ales with moderate to full bitterness and a naturally fruity character, stylistically ranging from best bitter to pale ale to IPA. Look for beers from a wide variety of hop-defined styles, such as Black Sheep Ale, County Durham Signature Ale, Sierra Nevada Pale Ale, and Anchor Liberty Ale.

Smoky—Ales and lagers with flavours ranging from a wisp of smoke to a raging campfire. Look for German rauchbiers, such as Aecht Schlenkerla Rauchbier; peated malt beers, such as Adelscott; or New World smoked malt beers, such as Alaskan Smoked Porter.

Spicy—Well-rounded ales with a natural spiciness, either from fermentation or a spice addition or both. Look for Belgian or Belgian-style strong blonde ales, such as La Fin du Monde and Westmalle Tripel, and complex North American spiced ales, such as Dogfish Head Midas Touch and AleSmith Grand Cru.

Robust—Rich and warming ales with a full maltiness and impressive complexity, and most often significant strength. Look for Scotch ales, such as Traquair House Ale; abbey and abbey-style ales, such as Rochefort 8 and Ommegang Ale; and rich and robust dark ales, such as North Coast Brother Thelonius.

Soothing—Potent ales with almost sinfully decadent maltiness and profound depth of flavour. Look for the biggest of the Belgian and Belgian-style ales, such as Chimay Grand Réserve, St. Bernardus Abt 12, and Lost Abbey Judgment Day, and sweeter Imperial stouts, such as Brooklyn Black Chocolate Stout.

Contemplative—Full-bodied lagers with full maltiness and refined character, principally full-flavoured, lager-fermented beers such as bocks and doppelbocks. Look for bocks, such as Einbecker Up-Bock Dunkel, and doppelbocks, such as Ayinger Celebrator and Samuel Adams Double Bock.

Fruity—Ales fermented or finished with real fruit or fruit juices. Look for almost anything with a fruit in its name, from Liefmans Framboise to Lindemans Pêche to Früli Strawberry Beer.

great beginnings

All good meals begin with beer or, if not, they should!
These flavour-filled creations are a great way to get a
dinner party started or, in some cases, can be comforting
and filling main courses for lunches or light dinners.

bistro salad

serve with: quenching

When we set out to devise a salad that would best reflect the restaurant, we wanted it to be unusual, bistro-y, and beer-dressed and to act as an appetizer or main course. We think this fits the bill, with the crunchy green beans, the sweet beets, and of course our delicious Lemon, White Beer, and Truffle Vinaigrette. To make a meal of it, add soft goat cheese, sautéed garlic shrimp, or grilled chicken or salmon.

- In a small saucepan over medium-high heat, add the beets and enough water to cover and bring to a boil. Cook beets until they are fork-tender, drain, and run under cold water to stop cooking. Peel and julienne beets on a mandolin or by hand.
- Cut tomatoes in half lengthwise, make a small incision lengthwise in the centre, scoop out seeds, press tomato meat flat against a cutting board, and julienne.
- Slice cucumber lengthwise in half and remove seeds. Cut lengthwise into pieces 2 inches (5 cm) long, then julienne.
- Wash all greens. Prepare frisée by breaking it into small pieces. Cut all but about 2 inches (5 cm) of the stems off watercress.
- Place all ingredients in a bowl except sprouts, add Lemon, White Beer, and Truffle Vinaigrette, and toss.
- Top salad with sprouts.

ingredients

1	medium red beet, julienned
1	medium yellow beet, julienned
2	Roma tomatoes, julienned
1/2	English cucumber, julienned
1 head	blonde frisée
1 bunch	watercress
3 cups (750 mL)	mesclun greens
1/4 cup (60 mL)	haricots verts (fine green beans), blanched
1 Tbsp (15 mL)	finely diced red onion
2 Tbsp (30 mL)	finely sliced (chiffonade) fresh basil
1 cup (250 mL)	Lemon, White Beer, and Truffle Vinaigrette (recipe, page 201)
1 box	pea or bean sprouts

serves 8

cured salmon salad
with pink grapefruit and pickled ginger vinaigrette

ingredients

1 head	frisée
1 head	Belgian endive
1 small handful	mesclun greens
1	grapefruit, segmented, membrane removed
1	small red onion, thinly sliced
1 cup (250 mL)	Pink Grapefruit and Pickled Ginger Vinaigrette (recipe, page 202)
1 lb (450 g)	White Beer–Cured Salmon, sliced (recipe, page 171)
2 Tbsp (30 mL)	capers, lightly deep-fried

serves 8

serve with: quenching or smoky

This is an ideal lunchtime salad, light enough not to be overly filling yet sufficiently substantial, thanks to the judicious use of salmon. As a dinner appetizer, it will wow your guests with a multitude of different but harmonious flavours.

- Wash all greens and dry thoroughly. Tear frisée into small pieces, separate endive into leaves, and combine with mesclun in a large salad bowl.
- Add grapefruit segments and sliced red onion.
- Dress salad with Pink Grapefruit and Pickled Ginger Vinaigrette and toss lightly.
- Top with White Beer–Cured Salmon and garnish with fried capers.

white beer–cured salmon
with sweet mustard and porter pancakes

serve with: quenching or satisfying

Taking traditional gravlax one step further and embracing Belgian white beer seems like a no-brainer to us. The orange and coriander in the beer complement the salmon perfectly. The moisture that a salt and sugar cure normally removes from the fish seems to be saved by the beer in this recipe, resulting in a uniquely silky texture.

- Begin by slicing the White Beer–Cured Salmon as thinly as possible, working from the head of the fish to the tail on a slight angle.
- Cook Porter Pancakes according to the recipe, making each about the size of a poker chip. Keep them warm.
- When you are ready to serve, place a slice or two of cured salmon on each pancake and top with some sliced onion and capers if desired.
- Finish with drizzle of Sweet Mustard Sauce right before serving.

ingredients

1 recipe	White Beer-Cured Salmon (recipe, page 171)
1 recipe	Porter Pancakes (recipe, page 200)
1	small red onion, thinly sliced
6 oz (180 g)	capers (optional)
1 recipe	Sweet Mustard Sauce (recipe, page 211)

serves 8–10

chicken liver–foie gras mousse

ingredients

6 oz (180 g)	chicken livers
	milk
2	egg yolks
1/2 cup (125 mL)	whipping (35%) cream
1 Tbsp (15 mL)	salt
pinch	freshly ground black pepper
1/2	clove garlic
2	sprigs fresh thyme, leaves removed and stems discarded
9 oz (250 g)	foie gras, cut into small cubes
1/3 cup (75 mL)	strong, malty, spicy ale (soothing)

special equipment

stainless-steel or non-reactive bowl

Blender

Fine strainer

2 oz (60 mL) Ramekins

Deep pan

serves 8

serve with: spicy

For some people, foie gras on its own is simply too rich, so we make it a little more approachable by adding some chicken livers to the mix. You still get all the decadent, delicious flavour of foie gras, but in a form that won't tax more delicate digestive systems.

- The day before cooking, place the chicken livers in a stainless-steel or non-reactive bowl and cover with milk to remove excess blood and impurities. Refrigerate overnight.
- When you're ready to make the mousse, preheat oven to 250°F (120°C).
- Drain livers and place in a blender with egg yolks and cream. Purée on high speed until smooth. Add salt, pepper, garlic, and thyme leaves and blend again.
- Cut foie gras into small cubes and, continuing to blend, add to the mixture a few at a time. Continue until all foie gras has been added and mixture is smooth.
- Add beer and continue to blend until smooth. At this point, mixture should resemble a milkshake.
- Strain mixture through a fine strainer and pour into ramekins.
- Place the ramekins in a deep pan and fill pan with hot water until it rises halfway up the sides of the ramekins, taking care not to splash water into mousse. Cover tightly with aluminum foil and bake for 20 minutes or until the mousse is set.

- Remove pan from oven and take out the ramekins immediately so they do not continue to cook in the hot water. Let cool at room temperature, then cover with plastic wrap or foil and refrigerate for up to 4 days.

steak tartare

ingredients

1/4 cup (60 mL)	finely chopped shallots
2 Tbsp (30 mL)	finely chopped dill pickle
2 Tbsp (30mL)	finely chopped capers
1	anchovy fillet, finely chopped
2 Tbsp (30mL)	finely chopped flat-leaf parsley
1/2 tsp (2 mL)	paprika
2 Tbsp (30 mL)	ketchup
1/2 Tbsp (7 mL)	Dijon mustard
1/2 tsp (2 mL)	Worcestershire sauce
1 Tbsp (15 mL)	olive oil
2 Tbsp (30 mL)	strong and malty dark ale (soothing)
pinch	salt and freshly ground black pepper
1 lb (450 g)	fresh tenderloin or flatiron steak, very cold
1	baguette, thinly sliced and toasted
	thinly sliced red onion (optional)
	freshly grated horseradish (optional)

special equipment

Large bowl

Chopped ice

Small metal bowl

serves 8

serve with: robust

Steak tartare is traditional French bistro fare. This tasty version is made exceptional by the addition of malty, strong ale. And since the beer helps keep the beef moist, you don't need to use as much oil as you would in some other recipes. The key to this, as for any steak tartare, is to keep the beef very cold until ready to use and chop it by hand, rather than using any mechanical equipment.

- Layer the bottom of a large bowl with chopped ice, then place a smaller metal bowl on top of the ice. (This will keep your ingredients very cold during preparation.)
- Place shallots, pickles, capers, chopped anchovy, and parsley into the chilled bowl. Add paprika, ketchup, mustard, and Worcestershire sauce, and mix well. Add oil, beer, salt, and pepper, and mix well. Taste and adjust seasoning if necessary.
- Remove steak from the refrigerator and, using a very sharp knife, slice it very thinly. Next, finely chop the slices, making sure to remove any visible fat along the way.
- Serve immediately with toast, thinly sliced red onion, and freshly grated horseradish as desired.

blonde ale pakoras
with roasted pineapple raita

serve with: crisp

While travelling in India, Brian discovered an incredible vegetarian restaurant and after dinner found that he could return the next day for a cooking class. Naturally, he did, and because of this he was able to bring the recipe for these pakoras back with him to Toronto. The only adjustment he made, naturally enough, was the addition of some Belgian-style blonde ale, which he says "makes the vegetables sing!"

- In a large mixing bowl, combine all ingredients except water and mix well until a thick paste is formed. Slowly add water until the paste becomes a thick batter. Let it rest at room temperature for 15-20 minutes.
- Meanwhile, preheat a deep fryer to 350°F (180°C).
- After batter has rested, recheck the consistency by frying one or two pakoras. If they come out heavy and cakey, add a little more water.
- With a small spoon—such as a teaspoon or very small ice cream scoop—drop small balls of batter into the fryer and fry until golden brown.
- Remove to paper towels and let cool, then taste the first couple of pakoras. If they seem heavy, adjust batter by adding a little more water.
- Continue frying until all batter is used or the desired number of pakoras has been made. Leftover batter can be stored, covered and refrigerated, for up to 5 days.
- Serve with Roasted Pineapple Raita or, if you like your food spicy, Roasted Pineapple Raita spiked with your favourite hot sauce.

ingredients

1 1/4 cup (300 mL)	chickpea flour
2 1/2 cup (625 mL)	Belgian-style blonde ale (spicy)
2/3 cup (150 mL)	roughly chopped Vidalia onions
2/3 cup (150 mL)	finely chopped cabbage
2/3 cup (150 mL)	cooked, thinly sliced potatoes
1/2 cup (125 mL)	grated yellow and green zucchini
1/4 cup (60 mL)	roughly chopped arugula
1/3 cup (75 mL)	finely chopped fresh mint
2 Tbsp (30 mL)	thinly sliced fresh basil
1 1/2 Tbsp (22 mL)	ground coriander
1 Tbsp (15 mL)	turmeric
1 Tbsp (15mL)	Indian red pepper (or red chili pepper)
1 tsp (5mL)	garam masala
1 Tbsp (15 mL)	Worcestershire sauce
2 Tbsp (30 mL)	salt
1/4 cup (60 mL)	water (if needed)
1 recipe	Roasted Pineapple Raita (recipe, page 199)

special equipment
Deep fryer

serves 8-10

baked oysters
with spicy cheese and stout

ingredients

18	fresh oysters
3 Tbsp (45 mL)	butter
1/4 cup (60 mL)	finely chopped shallots
1 Tbsp (15 mL)	finely diced garlic
1 bunch	watercress, washed, stemmed, and roughly chopped
1/2 lb (225 g)	baby spinach, washed and roughly chopped
2	jalapeño peppers, finely chopped
1 tsp (5 mL)	freshly ground black pepper
6 oz (180 g)	cream cheese
1/4 cup (60 mL)	stout (soothing)
1/4 cup (60 mL)	freshly grated Parmesan cheese

special equipment

Oyster knife

Food processor

serves 6

serve with: satisfying

When we were first presenting beerbistro's beer cuisine concept to a group of investors, Brian whipped up a massive backyard feast representing several examples of the kind of food he wanted to serve. No one can say for certain, but it's entirely possible that it was these oysters that cinched the deal.

- Preheat oven to 325°F (160°C).
- Rinse oysters well. Shuck and set oysters and their liquid aside, reserving the deep "cup" side of the shell for later use.
- In a large frying pan over medium heat, melt butter. Add shallots and garlic and sauté until soft and translucent. Add watercress, baby spinach, jalapeño, freshly ground black pepper, and juice from the oysters, and sauté until the greens are wilted. Remove from heat and let mixture cool.
- Place cream cheese in a food processor and process on medium speed. Continuing to process, slowly add beer until it is completely incorporated.
- Set oyster shells, cup-side up, on an ovenproof tray. Place small bed of spinach and watercress mixture on the bottom of each oyster cup. Top each with an oyster and a spoonful of cream cheese–beer mixture. Sprinkle with Parmesan cheese.
- Bake until the cheese mixture is light brown and bubbly, about 8 minutes. Serve immediately.

How to Shuck an Oyster

- Wash the outside of the shell in ice-cold water, removing all the dirt and barnacles.
- Wrap in a cloth so the oyster can't slip, and place on a cutting board.
- Hold the oyster with the deep, cup-shaped side of the shell on the bottom.
- Stick the point of an oyster knife into the hinge located at the narrowest point. Twist the knife side to side quite forcefully until the hinge breaks and you can slide your knife between the two shells.
- Twist the knife up and grab the top shell. Slide the knife along the top side of the shell right to the base to cut the muscle, and hold the meat to the shell. Make sure to slice along the shell so you cut the muscle and not through the delicate oyster meat.
- Remove the top shell, and keep the bottom upright so as not to lose any of the juices.
- Take the knife and cut under the other side of the muscle, scraping along the shell to release the oyster to move freely in its natural cup but leaving the oyster in place.
- Pick off any little pieces of shell, and smell the oyster to make sure there are no off odours.
- Arrange on a plate and serve.

beer-battered onion rings

ingredients

4	Vidalia onions
1 cup (250 mL)	cake and pastry flour
2 cups (500 mL)	cornstarch
3 Tbsp (45 mL)	baking powder
1/4 cup (60 mL)	kosher salt
2 1/2 cups (625 mL)	oatmeal stout (satisfying)

special equipment

Deep fryer

serves 10

serve with: bold or crisp

Everyone knows that beer adds greatly to anything battered, hence all the orders of beer-battered fish and chips served daily at bars and pubs around the world. We find that onion rings are just that much better when a little oatmeal stout is involved, especially when the rings come from big sweet Vidalia onions.

- Preheat a deep fryer to 350°F (180°C).
- Slice onions approximately 1 inch (2.5 cm) thick and separate into rings.
- In a mixing bowl, combine flour, cornstarch, baking powder, and salt. Whisk in beer until a batter forms, leaving some small lumps for texture.
- Dip onion rings into batter and fry until golden brown.
- Salt rings while they are still hot and serve immediately.

spicy beer-boiled shrimp

serve with: crisp

This is a simple and delicious appetizer that's sure to please. If desired, it can be made in advance up to the point that the shrimp are to be returned to the sauce—simply reheat the sauce on the stove, add the shrimp, and continue to heat until the shrimp are warmed through.

- In a large saucepan over high heat, melt 2 Tbsp (30 mL) butter. Add shallots and garlic and sauté until soft and translucent. Add leeks and red and yellow peppers and sauté until soft. Add tomatoes and garlic chile paste and cook until dry, about 1–2 minutes.
- Add shrimp and beer and bring to a boil. Then remove from the heat and let sit for 5 minutes.
- Remove shrimp and set aside.
- Return the pan to high heat and boil until reduced by 1/3. Add 2 Tbsp (30 mL) butter and stir until fully incorporated. Return shrimp to sauce until hot.
- Serve over crusty bread.

ingredients

1/2 cup (125 mL)	butter, divided
2 Tbsp (30 mL)	diced shallots
1 Tbsp (15 mL)	finely chopped garlic
1/4 cup (60 mL)	julienned leeks
1/4 cup (60 mL)	julienned red bell pepper
1/4 cup (60 mL)	julienned yellow bell pepper
2 Tbsp (15 mL)	thinly sliced (in rings) jalapeño pepper
1/4 cup (60 mL)	diced tomatoes
1 tsp (5 mL)	Asian garlic chile paste
1 lb (450 g)	raw jumbo shrimp, shelled and deveined
1/2 cup (125 mL)	pale ale (bold)
	crusty bread

serves 4–8

duck confit corn dogs

ingredients

3 cups (750 mL)	Duck Confit (recipe, page 168)
1/2 cup (125 mL)	duck fat
1 recipe	Corn Dog Batter (recipe, page 95)

special equipment

Food processor

Plastic wrap

16–20 Satay sticks

Deep fryer

serves 8–10

serve with: crisp, sociable, or bold

These grown-up versions of the carnival favourite are fun and tasty, and sure to evoke childhood memories.

- In a small saucepan over low heat, add Duck Confit and fat and stir gently until fat has melted and meat is warm.
- Remove meat from bone then transfer to a food processor and pulse very lightly until mixture has a shredded appearance.
- Roll meat into cylinders roughly the width of a hotdog, wrap tightly in plastic wrap, and place in the freezer.
- Once frozen, remove meat from the freezer, remove the plastic wrap, and cut into about 3 portions approximately 2 inches (5 cm) a piece. Slide a stick lengthwise into the centre of each duck confit tube so that the stick is roughly halfway in.
- Preheat deep fryer to 325°F (160°C).
- Dip duck confit sticks into Corn Dog Batter and blanch in the fryer until batter has firmed up and cooked but not taken on colour, approximately 2 minutes.
- Remove corn dogs from the fryer and let cool before the second frying. At this point, corn dogs can be wrapped in plastic wrap and stored in the refrigerator for up to 3 days. Be sure to allow them to come to room temperature before refrying.
- To finish, raise the temperature of the fryer to 350°F (180°C) and fry again until golden brown, about 4 minutes.

corn dog batter

- In a mixing bowl, combine flour, cornmeal, baking powder, salt, and sugar. Using your hands, mix in butter, rubbing it vigorously into flour until the texture is mealy. Make a well in the centre of the mixture and pour in egg, milk, and beer, then gently combine to create a smooth batter, drawing the flour mixture into the liquid a bit at a time.
- Allow batter to rest for 15 minutes. It should be quite thick, about the consistency of a soft paste, but if it is too runny or thick, adjust with a bit of flour or beer.

ingredients

1 1/3 cup (325 mL)	all-purpose flour
2/3 cup (150 mL)	yellow cornmeal
2 tsp (10 mL)	baking powder
2 tsp (10 mL)	salt
2 Tbsp (30 mL)	sugar
1/4 cup (60 mL)	butter, cut into small cubes
1	egg
1 cup (250 mL)	whole milk
1/2 cup (125 mL)	Belgian-style white beer (quenching)

makes enough batter to coat about 20 skewers of meat.

brown ale chili nachos

ingredients

40	nacho chips
1/4 lb (125 g)	cheddar cheese, grated, divided,
1/4 lb (125 g)	Monterey jack cheese, grated, divided
1/2 cup (125 mL)	Tomato-Avocado Salsa (recipe, page 198), divided
1 cup (250 mL)	Brown Ale Chili (recipe, page 192), divided
2 Tbsp (30 mL)	sliced jalapeño pepper, divided
2 Tbsp (30 mL)	sliced black olives, divided
1/4 cup (60 mL)	shredded lettuce
1/4 cup (60 mL)	Gueuze Sour Cream (recipe page 194)
2 Tbsp (30 mL)	sliced green onions
1/4 cup (60 mL)	chopped fresh tomatoes

special equipment
Ovenproof platter

makes enough nachos to fill a large platter.

serve with: bold

It was always a joke around the beerbistro kitchen that someday we'd add nachos to the menu, mainly because we didn't want to do the stereotypical "beer food," until one summer we decided to try it, just for fun. Somewhat to our chagrin, they were an instant hit and we had to take them off at the next menu change before they grew so popular that we would be stuck with them. A year later, customers were still asking for them.

- Preheat oven to 325°F (160°C).
- On an ovenproof platter, spread half of the nacho chips. Top chips with half of the cheese, Tomato-Avocado Salsa, and Brown Ale Chili. Place the rest of the chips on top and top with the remaining cheese, salsa, and chili. Scatter half of the jalapeño and olive slices over top.
- Bake until the cheese is melted, approximately 5–7 minutes.
- Remove from the oven and place hot platter on a room temperature platter to serve. Top with lettuce and Gueuze Sour Cream, then garnish with sprinkling of onions, chopped tomatoes, and the remaining jalapeño and olive slices.

curried butternut squash hummus

serve with: sociable

We've created a lot of dips and spreads in the beerbistro kitchen, but this remains a popular stalwart among a handful of others. Use it as a dip for pita wedges or pieces of grilled flatbread, or add it to a favourite sandwich or spiced chicken burger.

- Preheat oven to 325°F (160°C).
- On the middle rack of the oven, roast squash until cooked through, approximately 45 minutes.
- Meanwhile, in a medium saucepan over medium heat, add oil, and sauté onions with curry paste until soft. Remove from heat and set aside.
- When squash is cool enough to handle, scrape flesh from the skin and put flesh in the bowl of a food processor. Add chickpeas and process until almost smooth. Add remaining ingredients and blend until smooth.
- Taste and adjust seasoning as needed. Serve immediately or store, covered, in the refrigerator for up to 5 days.

ingredients

1/2	butternut squash, cut in 2 pieces, seeds removed
2 Tbsp (30 mL)	vegetable oil
1/2	small sweet onion, finely diced
2 Tbsp (30 mL)	mild curry paste
1 can (28 oz/796 mL)	chickpeas, drained
1/4 cup (60 mL)	tahini
2 tsp (10 mL)	chopped garlic
2 Tbsp (30 mL)	roasted garlic
1/4 cup (60 mL)	best bitter (bold)
1 Tbsp (15 mL)	olive oil
2 Tbsp (30 mL)	freshly squeezed lemon juice
1/4 tsp (1 mL)	cayenne pepper
pinch	salt and freshly ground black pepper

special equipment

Food processor

makes 4 cups (1 L)

spicy kobe beef and beer tacos

ingredients

1 cup (250 mL)	adzuki beans (small red beans)
1 Tbsp (15 mL)	vegetable oil
2 1/4 cups (560 mL)	onions, finely diced
2 lbs (900 g)	Kobe beef knuckle, shaved thinly
pinch	salt and freshly ground black pepper
2 tsp (10 mL)	ground cumin
4	cloves garlic, chopped
1 tsp (5 mL)	granulated sugar
1/4 cup (60 mL)	chili powder
1 can (28 oz/796 mL)	diced tomatoes, with juice
2 1/4 cups (560 mL)	malty golden lager (sociable)
3	chile peppers
1 tsp (5 mL)	red hot sauce
1 tsp (5 mL)	salt

makes 12 tacos

served with: bold

Okay, we admit that tacos (and nachos) are not exactly classic "bistro" cuisine, but we think that having fun with your food is important too. And judging by the way our customers have responded to these beefy, hearty treats, they're inclined to agree. If you want to go with a less expensive cut of beef, make sure you simmer the beef and bean mixture until the meat is as tender as can be.

- Place beans in a large bowl, cover with cold water, and let soak in the refrigerator overnight. (If you're using canned beans, omit this step.) Drain when ready to use.
- In a deep pan or heavy-bottomed pot over medium heat, heat oil. Add onions and beef and cook until browned. Season with salt and pepper and add cumin, garlic, sugar, and chili powder. Mix well. Add tomato sauce, beer, chile peppers, hot sauce, and salt. Bring to a boil and reduce to a simmer. Cook for approximately 90 minutes.
- Add beans and continue to cook until they are tender and chili is the desired "wetness," about 15 minutes. If the mixture is too dry, add a little more beer or some water.

to build the taco:

- In the bottom of each taco shell, place some shredded lettuce. Add a thin layer of grated cheese.

- Top with chili and garnish with Gueuze Sour Cream and grilled onions.

ingredients

12	taco shells
2 cups (500 mL)	finely shredded iceberg lettuce,
2 cups (500 mL)	grated gouda
1/2 cup (125 mL)	Gueuze Sour Cream (recipe, page 194)
1	medium onion, sliced and grilled with a little oil, salt, and freshly ground black pepper

honey brown chicken wings

ingredients

5 lbs (2.25 kg)	jumbo chicken wings
12 oz (355 mL)	honey brown ale (sociable), divided
1/4 cup (60 mL)	Dijon mustard, divided
1/4 cup (60 mL)	liquid honey, divided
1 Tbsp (15 mL)	Barbeque Spice Rub (see sidebar below)

special equipment

Barbeque

rub ingredients

8 oz (225 g)	granulated sugar
4 oz (110 g)	kosher salt
2 oz (60 mL)	celery salt
3 oz (90 mL)	paprika
1 1/4 oz (36 g)	freshly ground black pepper
1 1/2 oz (42 g)	ground cumin
1/3 oz (10 g)	dry mustard
1/2 oz (15 g)	onion powder
1 1/2 oz (42 g)	granulated garlic
1/2 oz (15 g)	chili powder
1/8 oz (4 g)	cayenne pepper

serves 8

serve with: crisp

Beer, honey, and spice give these chicken wings just the right balance with the charred flavour of the barbeque in this carefree summer lip-smacking dish.

- In a large bowl or sealable plastic bag, marinate chicken wings in half of the honey brown ale, Dijon mustard, and honey for at least 24 hours before grilling.
- Preheat barbeque or grill to medium-high.
- Grill chicken wings on barbeque or grill, turning every 3 to 4 minutes, until wings are golden brown and crispy, approximately 10–12 minutes.
- Place in a large bowl and add remaining honey brown, Dijon, and honey to the bowl. Toss until wings are thoroughly and evenly coated.
- Sprinkle on your favourite barbeque spice rub and toss again. Serve immediately.

barbeque spice rub

This my favourite rub for chicken or pork. You must weigh all these ingredients.

- Combine all the spices and mix thoroughly.
- Keep in a dry, sealed container and use as necessary.

cold spring pea soup with
white beer, yogurt, crushed red peppercorns, and mint

serve with: quenching

This dish is so light and refreshing, it's like having summer in a soup bowl. For best results, use early fresh peas, but don't let a lack of them dissuade you from trying this soup—it's still a treat when you use frozen peas!

- In a heavy-bottomed medium saucepan over medium heat, melt butter. Add leeks and onions and cook, stirring constantly, until softened, about 5 minutes.
- Add 4 cups (1 L) of beer and bring to a boil. Reduce heat and simmer for 10 minutes.
- Add peas and transfer immediately to a food processer or blender (or use an immersion blender) and purée.
- Pass soup through a fine strainer and chill until ready to use.
- When well chilled, add orange juice, mint, crushed peppercorns, and remaining beer to the soup. (This portion of beer is left uncooked so its natural carbonation will lighten the taste of the soup and enhance its elegance).
- Ladle soup into chilled soup bowls and top with a spoonful of yogurt. The soup can be refrigerated for up to 3 days before serving.

Note: There is a notable absence of salt in this dish because Belgian-style wheats don't generally marry well with salt. If you find the taste too flat, add a little more orange juice for added zest.

ingredients

1 Tbsp (15 mL)	unsalted butter
2 cups (500 mL)	diced leeks
1 cup (250 mL)	diced Spanish onion
4 1/2 cups (1.125 L)	Belgian-style white beer (quenching), divided
4 1/2 cups (1.125 L)	fresh peas or 2 lb (1 kg) bag frozen peas
1/4 cup (60 mL)	freshly squeezed orange juice
1 tsp (5 mL)	finely julienned fresh mint
1/2 tsp (2 mL)	crushed red peppercorns
1/4 cup (60 mL)	plain yogurt

special equipment

Food processer, blender, or immersion blender.

serves 8–10

butternut squash and ale soup

ingredients

3 Tbsp (45 mL)	butter
2	medium Spanish onions, finely diced
1	medium butternut squash, peeled, seeded, and cut into 1-inch (2.5 cm) cubes
4 1/2 cups (1.125 L)	chicken stock
1 1/2 cups (375 mL)	whipping (35%) cream
1 1/2 cups (375 mL)	grated aged farmhouse cheddar
12 oz (355 mL)	cream ale (sociable)
1 Tbsp (15 mL)	salt
1 tsp (5 mL)	freshly ground black pepper

special equipment

Food processor, blender, or immersion blender

serves 8–10

serve with: satisfying

Whereas most squash soups are typically winter fare, we like this soup regardless of the season. That's because of the light hoppy zip the cream ale brings to the dish.

- In a large, heavy-bottomed saucepan over medium heat, melt butter. Add onions and cook until transparent.
- Add butternut squash and cook, stirring, for 5 minutes.
- Add chicken stock and bring to a boil. Reduce heat and simmer for approximately 20 minutes or until squash is very tender.
- Transfer to a food processor or blender (or use an immersion blender) and purée until completely smooth.
- Return soup to the pot and add cream. Bring to a boil. Reduce heat to a simmer and whisk in the cheddar cheese. Keeping the soup at a simmer, whisk in the beer. Adjust seasoning with a pinch of salt and pepper, and serve.

butterbean and lager soup

serve with: soothing

This is a wonderful autumn or winter soup, perfect for cool nights and short days. For more comfort, add a dollop of sour cream to each bowl and serve with plenty of toasted and buttered crusty bread.

- In a large bowl, cover dry beans with cold water. Let soak in the refrigerator overnight. (If using canned beans, omit this step.) Drain well when ready to use.
- In a large, heavy-bottomed saucepan over medium heat, melt butter. Add onion, leek, fennel, and carrot and sauté until soft. Add garlic and continue to cook until fragrant, taking care not to brown the vegetables.
- Add beans, beer, stock, and pork to the saucepan, and bring to a boil. Reduce heat to a simmer and cook until beans are soft, skimming off any foam that rises to the top.
- When beans are tender, add fresh herbs and season with salt and pepper.

ingredients

1/2 cup (125 mL)	dried butterbeans (or lima beans)
2 Tbsp (30 mL)	unsalted butter
1	small onion, diced
1	leek, finely diced
1/2	bulb fennel, finely diced
1/4 cup (60 mL)	finely diced carrot
2	cloves garlic, finely chopped
1 1/4 cup (300 mL)	malty golden lager (sociable)
3 1/2 cups (825 mL)	chicken stock
1/2	smoked pork hock, roughly diced in bite-sized pieces off the bone
2	sprigs fresh thyme, leaves removed and chopped, stems discarded
1 Tbsp (15 mL)	chopped fresh basil
1 Tbsp (15 mL)	chopped fresh flat-leaf parsley
pinch	salt and freshly ground black pepper

serves 8–10

onion and mushroom soup
with scotch ale and blue cheese

ingredients

1/3 cup (75 mL)	duck fat or butter
6 cups (1.5 L)	sliced sweet onions (about 5 medium onions)
8 oz (225 g)	portobello mushrooms, sliced
6 oz (180 g)	shiitake mushrooms, sliced
2 1/4 cups (550 mL)	Scotch ale (robust)
2 1/4 cups (550 mL)	veal stock
4 1/2 cups (1.125 L)	chicken stock
4	sprigs thyme, leaves removed and stems discarded
pinch	salt and freshly ground freshly ground black pepper
1–2	baguettes, thinly sliced and toasted (20–30 pieces)
2 cups (500 mL)	shredded or grated mozzarella
8 oz (125 g)	blue cheese, crumbled

serves 10

serve with: satisfying or smoky

French onion soup is a bistro classic, but we thought it would be a little cheeky to keep that name when we use Scotch ale in its creation! Nevertheless, it lives up to its pedigree as a comforting fall, winter, or early spring soup that, depending on your appetite, could be served as a starter or main dish.

- In a large, heavy-bottomed saucepan over very low heat, melt duck fat. Add onions and portobello and shiitake mushrooms and cook until soft and lightly coloured. This should take approximately 4 hours.
- When vegetables are ready, add ale, veal stock, and chicken stock and bring to a boil.
- Stir in thyme leaves and reduce the heat. Simmer for 30 minutes or until all the flavours have developed. Season to taste and remove from heat. At this point, soup can be stored in the refrigerator for up to 6 days and reheated when ready to serve.
- When ready to serve, preheat broiler and fill onion soup bowls about three-quarters full and top with a layer of toasted bread. Top with mozzarella, then blue cheese.
- Place under broiler for 3–5 minutes or until the cheese has melted and browned a little. Serve immediately.

everyday delicious

When we opened beerbistro, we wanted to serve not
only beer cuisine but also comforting beer cuisine, the kind
of food that just makes you feel good about eating it. The
recipes in this section are perhaps the best illustration of
that sort of fare.

lobster quesadilla

serve with: crisp

We started making these for fun one summer, thinking they were such an obvious, upscale take on classic chicken or pork quesadillas that our regular customers would get a kick out of them. Little did we know they'd prove so popular that we haven't been able to take them off the menu since!

- Preheat oven to 425°F (220°C).
- If using fresh lobster meat, check that any cartilage is removed from claw meat.
- Butter one side of each tortilla and place, butter side down. On one half of each tortilla, scatter half the smoked cheddar, tomato, red and green onion, bacon, coriander, and basil. Top with half the lobster meat, making sure to cover the surface evenly. Cover with the other half of the tortilla and press firmly to seal.
- Place both tortillas on a baking sheet and bake for 5 minutes. Turn over and continue baking for another 2 minutes. At this point, quesadillas should be golden brown. If they're not, turn on the broiler and grill until golden brown. Watch that they don't burn.
- Chop each quesadilla into 4 wedges and serve with Tomato-Avocado Salsa (recipe, page 198) and Gueuze Sour Cream (recipe, page 194).

ingredients

6 oz (180 g)	lobster meat, fresh or canned, and picked over for shells
2 Tbsp (30 mL)	butter, softened
2	12-inch (30 cm) flour tortillas
1 cup (250 mL)	grated smoked cheddar
1/4 cup (60 mL)	diced Roma tomato
1/4 cup (60 mL)	finely diced red onion
1/4 cup (60 mL)	finely diced green onion
1/4 cup (60 mL)	bacon, cooked until crisp and finely chopped
1/4 cup (60 mL)	chopped fresh coriander leaves
1/4 cup (60 mL)	finely sliced (chiffonade) fresh basil

serves 2

drunken portobello
mushroom sandwich

ingredients

8 oz (225 g)	portobello mushrooms
3/4 cup (175 mL)	stout, (satisfying)
3/4 cup (175 mL)	balsamic vinegar
1/4	bunch fresh thyme, leaves removed and stems discarded
1/4	bunch fresh rosemary
pinch	salt and freshly ground black pepper,
2	Buttermilk-Beer Buns (recipe, page 243)
1/2 cup (125 mL)	Curried Butternut Squash Hummus (recipe, page 97)
1/2 cup (125 mL)	arugula
1	red bell pepper, roasted and cut into strips
1/4 cup (60 mL)	goat cheese

serves 2

serve with: satisfying or smoky

Portobello mushrooms, with their firm texture and earthy taste, are the vegetarian's steak. So it's hardly a surprise that they pair brilliantly with beer, both in the marinade and at the table. These are veggie sandwiches even the most committed meat eater will love.

- In a large bowl, toss mushrooms with stout, vinegar, thyme, rosemary, salt, and pepper. Marinate for about 20 minutes.
- Meanwhile, preheat grill, if using.
- Remove mushrooms from marinade and drain off any remaining liquid. Sauté in a hot frying pan or grill until tender but not shrivelled.
- Cut each Buttermilk-Beer Bun in half and spread one side with half of the Curried Butternut Squash Hummus. Top with a few arugula leaves and half the red pepper strips. Place half of the mushrooms on top of pepper strips.
- Spread the other side of each bun with half of the goat cheese and place on top of mushroom side. Press firmly.
- Butter or oil the outside of bun then fry sandwiches in a frying pan over medium heat or in a sandwich press.

grilled porter-braised
pulled pork quesadilla

serve with: bold

More traditional than our lobster quesadillas, these beauties are every bit as popular, and just one of the many delicious ways you can make use of our Porter-Braised Pulled Pork.

- Preheat grill to medium-high.
- Lay out tortillas and spread 1/2 Tbsp (7 mL) of butter evenly on each. Turn over 4 of the tortillas and divide Porter-Braised Pulled Pork evenly among them, spreading it out to cover the whole tortilla. Top evenly with the green onions and cheese. Top with another tortilla, buttered side up.
- On a hot grill, working in batches if necessary, grill tortillas until one side is golden brown. Turn over and continue to grill until both sides are crisp and brown.
- Remove to a cutting board and cut each quesadilla into 8 even wedges. Serve with Tomato-Avocado Salsa and sour cream.

ingredients

1/4 cup (60 mL)	butter, divided
8	12-inch (30 cm) flour tortillas
1 pound (450 g)	Porter-Braised Pulled Pork (recipe, page 177)
1/2 cup (125 mL)	sliced green onions
2 cups (500 mL)	grated Monterey Jack cheese (approx. 8 oz /225 g)
2 cups (500 mL)	Tomato-Avocado Salsa (recipe, page 198)
1 cup (250 mL)	sour cream

serves 8

drunken spaghetti
with clams and stout

ingredients

2 Tbsp (30 mL)	olive oil
1	medium onion, sliced
1	red bell pepper, julienned
4	jalapeño peppers, thinly sliced
1 1/2 cups (375 mL)	chicken stock
1 tsp (5 mL)	crushed hot pepper flakes
1 tsp (5 mL)	Worcestershire sauce
1 can (14 oz/398 mL)	baby clams (meat and juice)
12 oz (375 g)	spaghetti
1/2 cup (60 mL)	pesto
6 oz. (180 mL)	stout (satisfying)
1/4 cup (60 mL)	vodka
1/4 cup (60 mL)	butter
1/2 cup (125 mL)	freshly grated Parmesan cheese
1	bunch fresh flat-leaf parsley, chopped

serves 4–6

serve with: crisp or satisfying

Shellfish and stout are such great friends, we can hardly be blamed for wanting to add our beer cuisine twist to an Italian classic (spaghetti alle vongole).

- In a large, heavy-bottomed saucepan over medium-high, add olive oil, onion, and peppers. Sauté until onion is soft and fragrant, about 3 minutes.
- Add chicken stock, hot pepper flakes, Worcestershire sauce, and clam juice. Bring to a boil and reduce until almost dry.
- While sauce is reducing, cook spaghetti until al dente in a large saucepan of boiling salted water.
- Reduce the heat under the sauce and add clams, pesto, and stout, taking care not to boil the liquid, which will cook the cheese in the pesto.
- Stir in cooked spaghetti, vodka, butter, cheese, and parsley until the cheese and butter have melted. Serve immediately.

Note: If you want to use fresh clams for this dish, steam 2 lbs (1 kg) of clams in their own juice and reserve the liquid the clams leave behind in the pot. Shell clams and add the meat with its reserved liquid as above.

coq au bier
with sour cream dumplings

ingredients

2 Tbsp (15 mL)	oil
8	chicken legs, separated into drums and thighs
1 tsp (5 mL)	coarse salt
1/2 tsp (2 mL)	freshly ground black pepper
2 Tbsp (30 mL)	butter
4 oz (110 g)	bacon, cut horizontally into strips
1	small sweet onion, finely diced
1 cup (250 mL)	pearl onions
8 oz (225 g)	crimini mushrooms, sliced
4 oz (110 mL)	portobello mushrooms, sliced
2 cups (500 mL)	nut brown ale (sociable)
1 cup (250 mL)	chicken stock
1/4 cup (60 mL)	whipping (35%) cream
1 Tbsp (15 mL)	chopped fresh tarragon
24	Gueuze Sour Cream Dumplings (recipe, page 194)
pinch	salt and freshly gound black pepper

serves 8

serve with: sociable or bold

The inspiration of this dish came from Paul Bocuse, a master chef of classic French cuisine. We just gave coq au vin a beer twist. After trying the dish with a multitude of different beers, we discovered that nut brown ale harmonized best. This dish has become a trademark cold-weather favourite.

- Preheat oven to 350°F (180°C).
- In a large, heavy-bottomed frying pan over medium heat, heat oil. Season chicken parts with salt and pepper and sauté in hot oil until browned. Remove and drain excess oil.
- Return the pan to the heat and melt butter. Sauté bacon until fat has been rendered.
- Add onions and mushrooms and sauté until soft. Return chicken to the pan, add beer and chicken stock, and bring to a boil.
- Remove from heat and cover tightly with lid or aluminum foil. Continue to cook in the preheated oven for 1 hour or until chicken is cooked through.
- All steps to this point can be done up to a day in advance and the chicken stored in the refrigerator until ready to use.
- When ready to serve, place chicken and broth over medium heat on the stovetop and reheat gently. Stir in cream and tarragon and top with Gueze Sour Cream dumplings. Reduce liquid until broth is thick enough to coat the back of a wooden spoon, or about 2 minutes. Adjust seasoning with a pinch salt and pepper, and serve.

kriek-braised rabbit

ingredients

2	rabbits
1 Tbsp (15 mL)	butter
1 Tbsp (15 mL)	oil
2 oz (60 g)	bacon, cut horizontally into strips
4	shallots, diced
1	white onion, sliced
1/2 lb (225 g)	cremini mushrooms, quartered
1/2 lb (225 g)	portobello mushrooms, sliced
16 oz (2 cups/ 500 mL)	kriek (fruity)
1 cup (250 mL)	chicken stock
1/4 cup (60 mL)	whipping (35%) cream
2 Tbsp (30 mL)	chopped fresh tarragon

special equipment
Boning knife

serves 8

serve with: contemplative or fruity

Our variation on the Flemish classic of rabbit cooked in gueuze adds the element of fruitiness from the cherries used in the kriek. Usually, we're purists where lambic beers are concerned, preferring the tart, traditional examples of the style, but in this case we find that a kriek with some fruity sweetness adds to the soothing, comfort-food nature of the dish. This recipe goes well with Mustard Seed Spaetzle (recipe, page 195).

- Remove legs and meat along the ribs of the rabbit. Chop legs in half. (You can ask your butcher to do this for you.)
- Preheat oven to 325°F (160°C).
- Place a large, deep frying pan over medium-high heat and heat butter and oil. Sauté rabbit pieces in batches if necessary to avoid over-crowding until nicely browned.
- Remove rabbit and lower the heat to medium. Add bacon and cook until fat has been rendered. Stir in shallots, onions, and mushrooms and sauté until soft.
- Return rabbit pieces to the pan and stir in the kriek, chicken stock, and cream. Bring to a boil.
- Cover the pan tightly with a lid or aluminum foil and place in the preheated oven to cook until rabbit is tender, about 2 hours.
- All steps to this point can be done up to a day in advance and the rabbit stored in the refrigerator until ready to use.
- When ready to serve, remove rabbit from the broth and set aside. Place pan on stove over medium heat and bring liquid to a boil. Reduce until thick enough to lightly coat the back of a wooden spoon.
- Reduce heat to medium-low, return rabbit pieces to sauce, and simmer until meat is warmed through. Stir in tarragon and serve.

white beer–poached salmon

There's something about Belgian-style white beer and salmon that we find make them naturals together. This simple but delectable recipe makes full and delicious use of this relationship.

- Preheat oven to 325°F (160°C).
- Place a deep frying pan over medium heat, melt butter, and sauté leeks until soft. Add garlic and sauté until fragrant, about 45 seconds. Add cream and bring to a boil. Continue to cook until the sauce is reduced by about half its original volume.
- Stir in beer, then fillets, stirring so sauce, leeks, and garlic cover all the pieces of salmon. Cover with a tight-fitting lid or aluminum foil and finish the cooking in the oven until the salmon is just cooked, about 12–14 minutes.
- Remove salmon and cover with foil to keep warm.
- Return the pan to the stove over high heat and bring quickly to a boil. Reduce until the sauce is still thin but lightly coats the back of a wooden spoon.
- Squeeze in lemon juice and add chopped parsley. Taste sauce and season with salt and pepper if desired.
- Serve the fillets one to a plate and top with the sauce, being sure to get a fair amount of leeks on each piece. Serve with seasonal vegetables and rice or potatoes if desired.

ingredients

1 Tbsp (15 mL)	butter
1/2 cup (125 mL)	diced leeks
2 tsp (10 mL)	chopped garlic
1/2 cup (125 mL)	whipping (35%) cream
1/2 cup (125 mL)	Belgian-style white beer (quenching)
4 fillets (each 6 oz/ 180 g)	Atlantic salmon
1	lemon wedge
2 tsp (10 mL)	chopped fresh parsley
pinch	salt and freshly ground black pepper

serves 4

ale-braised veal cheeks

ingredients

5 lbs (2.25 kg)	veal cheeks
pinch	salt and freshly ground black pepper
1/2 cup (125 mL)	oil
6	sprigs fresh thyme, leaves removed and stems discarded
2 sprigs	fresh rosemary, leaves removed and stems discarded
2–3	juniper berries
3	cloves garlic
2 cups (500 mL)	De Koninck Ale or similar sociable beer
1 Tbsp (15 mL)	red wine vinegar
4 1/2 cups (1.125 L)	veal stock

serves 8

serve with: robust

During the first few years of beerbistro's existence, cheeks suddenly became the meat du jour, with everything from halibut to beef cheeks popping up on our menu. Fortunately, we were already hip to the appeal of these tender, oh-so-tasty morsels and answered the trend with this riff on cheeks braised in Belgian ale.

- Season veal cheeks well with salt and pepper.
- Preheat oven to 275°F (140°C).
- In a large, deep, heavy-bottomed frying pan over medium-high heat, heat oil until very hot but not smoking. Add veal cheeks and brown on all sides.
- Remove meat from the pan and drain excess oil. Reduce heat to medium and return cheeks to the pan along with rosemary, thyme, juniper berries, garlic, beer, and vinegar.
- In a separate medium saucepan, bring veal stock to a boil and pour over cheeks.
- Cover the pan with a lid or foil and continue to cook in the oven for 6 hours or until a knife passes easily through the cheeks.
- Remove cheeks from the pan and set aside. Pass liquid through a strainer to remove solids. Skim if necessary.
- Return liquid to the pan over medium-high heat and reduce until it thickens and lightly coats the back of a spoon. Reduce heat and return cheeks to sauce. Heat gently until cheeks are warmed through.
- Serve over mashed potatoes or sweet potato mash with seasonal vegetables, or over ravioli or other pasta in a butter or light cream sauce.

port and stout–braised
lamb shanks

ingredients

8	lamb shanks (ask your butcher to peel and trim them for you)
pinch	salt and freshly ground black pepper
2 cups (500 mL)	flour
1/4 cup (125 mL)	olive oil
2	medium onions, finely diced
2 Tbsp (30 mL)	roughly chopped garlic
1/2 cup (125 mL)	port wine
4	Roma tomatoes, quartered and seeded
2	carrots, diced (about 1 cup/250 mL)
2	parsnips, diced (about 1 cup/250 mL)
2 cups (500 mL)	stout (satisfying)
1 cup (250 mL)	veal jus or reduced chicken or beef stock
1 Tbsp (15 mL)	Dijon mustard
1/4 cup (60 mL)	chopped fresh flat-leaf parsley

serves 8

serve with: robust or soothing

Lamb shanks are a wonderful and inexpensive way to bring the full flavour of spring lamb to your table, and because most of the work is done ahead of time, this recipe is ideal for entertaining. Plus, you can surprise your guests with a few bottles of Trappist or abbey-style ale in place of the red wine.

- Preheat oven to 325°F (160°C).
- Season shanks with salt and pepper and roll in flour until well coated.
- In a large saucepan over medium-high heat, heat oil until very hot but not smoking. Add shanks and brown well on all sides.
- Remove shanks from the saucepan and reduce heat to medium. Add onions and garlic and sauté until onions become translucent. Add port and deglaze the pan, using a wooden spoon to scrape any bits off the bottom.
- Stir in tomatoes, carrots and parsnips, then stout and veal jus.
- Return shanks to the pan and stir so lamb is covered as much as possible with the liquid and vegetables. Cover the pot with a tight-fitting lid or aluminum foil and continue to cook in the oven for 2–2 1/2 hours or until lamb is fork-tender.
- Using a large slotted spoon, remove shanks and vegetables from the pot and set aside. Strain remaining liquid through a fine sieve into a clean empty saucepan. Reduce over medium-high heat until resulting jus lightly coats the back of a wooden spoon. Remove from heat and skim off any fat that might appear on the surface.

- Stir mustard and parsley into jus.
- For each plate, make a mound of mashed potatoes, sweet potato mash, or other starch and surround it with vegetables from the pot. Place one shank in the centre and drizzle jus over top. Serve immediately.

belgian ale steak stew

serve with: robust or soothing

Known on the menu as Maudite Beef Stew, simply because we make it with Unibroue's fine Maudite Ale, this has been a customer favourite from the moment it first appeared at beerbistro. It's so popular, in fact, that when we take it off the menu in spring, complaints inevitably follow, even though we see this as much more a cold-weather dish than summertime fare. Another dish that's great for entertaining, this actually improves if made a day or two in advance.

- Preheat oven to 350°F (180°C).
- Dice steak into 1-inch (2.5 cm) cubes, removing any sinew.
- In a large bowl, combine flour and salt and pepper. Toss beef cubes in flour until all are evenly coated.
- In a deep heavy-bottomed frying pan over medium heat, melt butter. Add beef cubes, browning each on all sides and working in batches if necessary to avoid overcrowding.
- Remove from pan and add onions. Sauté until soft. Add tomato paste and continue to cook until onions have become a rust colour.
- Return beef to the pan and add mustard and beer. Stir well. Bring the stew to a simmer, then cook in the oven for 1 hour.
- Serve with Frites (recipe, page 150) or mashed potatoes and vegetables.

ingredients

2 1/4 lbs (1 kg)	top sirloin
1/2 cup (125 mL)	all-purpose flour
pinch	salt and freshly ground black pepper
1/2 cup (125 mL)	butter
8	medium red onions, diced
1 Tbsp (15 mL)	tomato paste
2 Tbsp (30 mL)	Dijon mustard
4 1/2 cups (1.125 L)	malty or spicy Belgian or Belgian-style ale (robust or spicy)

serves 8

mussels, mussels, and more mussels

(plus our frites)

A Word about Mussels

Everyone seems to love mussels. When the steaming and fragrant pot arrives at the table, almost anyone within smelling distance instantly takes note. Then the lid comes off, and the colours and aromas become almost too potent to resist. Adding to those mouth-watering flavours and fragrances, of course, is the simple, almost primitive joy of getting hands-on with your food, which really is the only way to properly eat steamed mussels.

On an average day at beerbistro, we serve more than fifty pounds of sweet, plump mussels, which we have flown in from the East Coast twice weekly. Comparable mussels should be available locally from any decent fishmonger.

Buying, Storing, and Cleaning

When buying mussels, remember that they're living animals and that the warmer their environment, the higher their metabolism and the faster they'll perish. So buy only mussels that are kept on ice and, if unfamiliar with the store, ask how long ago the latest shipment was received. Pick over the mussels before buying to make sure you don't get any with cracked or seriously chipped shells or, if open, any that don't close up when lightly squeezed.

Under the right conditions, mussels can live out of the water for up to twelve days, which, given that they're likely about three to five days old when you buy them, means that you have about a week before they start to expire. To keep them plump, juicy, and healthy, it's important to follow proper storage techniques.

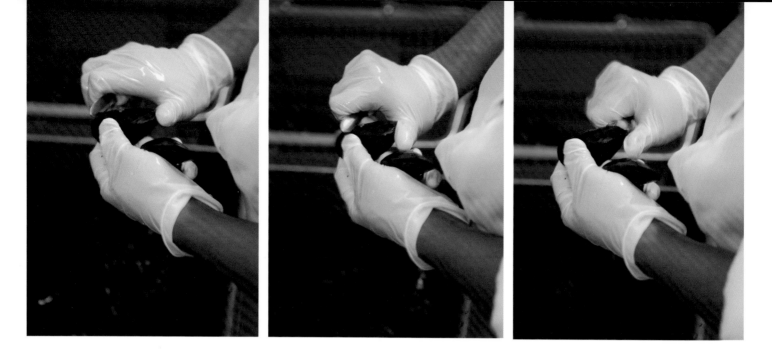

Mussels can breathe only if they're in a cool, moist environment and their gills are kept wet. Like any animal, they can't breathe if they're kept in closed plastic bags or airtight containers, and they don't take well to sitting in stagnant water, so proper drainage is a must. So the best way to store them is in the refrigerator, in a strainer hooked over the top of a bowl and covered with a damp cloth and some ice.

Never clean your mussels until you're ready to cook them, or you might do damage and cause them to die before cooking. Rinse them well in plenty of cold water, discarding any that have cracked or chipped shells or won't close when lightly squeezed. (They don't need to snap shut, just so long as you see movement when you squeeze the shell gently or give it a sharp thwack with the back of a spoon or the handle of a knife.) Pull off the fibrous "beards" by yanking them backward toward the hinge of the shell, and knock off any barnacles with a paring knife. Finally, give the shells a final scrub to remove any clinging bits of dirt or shell.

Cooking

When steaming mussels, always use a large pan to ensure you have plenty of room to move the the mussels around, and make sure the pan is very hot before adding any ingredients. (If the mussels are overcrowded, the ones on the bottom will overcook before those on top open.) Try to use a pot with a lid that seals tightly, and be sure to shake the pan regularly to move the mussels about and keep them cooking evenly. Keep cooking only until they open up—about 3 to 4 minutes. Any longer and the meat will shrivel and fall out of the shell.

Serving

One of the great things about eating mussels with friends is that it's like family-style dining even if you each have your own pot or bowl. Experienced mussel eaters will use an empty shell as their only utensil, but it's still nice to offer everyone a fork just in case.

Belgian-style fries, known as frites, are the classic accompaniment for steamed mussels, but whether you serve them or not, lots of good crusty bread is essential. How else are people going to sop up the delicious broth at the bottom of their bowls?
Cooked mussels that are left over can be shelled and preserved in oil and vinegar and stored, covered, in the fridge for an additional 7 days. Tossing a few on top of a green salad is an excellent way to make use of them.

belgian white mussels

ingredients

2 Tbsp (30 mL)	butter
1 1/2 Tbsp (22 mL)	chopped garlic
2 pounds (900 g)	mussels
1/2	lemon, cut into wedges
6 Tbsp (90 mL)	Belgian white beer (quenching)
1/4 cup (60 mL)	whipping (35%) cream
3 Tbsp (15 mL)	chopped fresh flat-leaf parsley
pinch	salt

serves 2–4

serve with: quenching or crisp

If you like garlic and cream, these are sure to be your favourite mussels, as they have been for many of our customers since they first appeared on our menu. The white beer adds a delicate complexity of citrus and coriander to the dish, while the lemon juice lightens and balances the garlic, cream, and butter.

- Heat a shallow sauté pan until very hot. Melt butter and sauté garlic until soft and fragrant, approximately 1 minute. Add cleaned mussels and give a good shake. Squeeze the juice from wedges of lemon over the mussels and cook for 30 seconds.
- Add beer and cream, give another shake, cover, and steam mussels for 3 minutes or until mussels just start to open.
- Add parsley, give another shake, and let boil with the cover off to reduce sauce, approximately 1 minute. Discard any shells that do not open fully during cooking. Taste and season with salt, if needed.
- Serve immediately in one large or four individual warmed bowls and pour almost all the liquid over the mussels, watching for and avoiding the grit that may sit in the last spoonful or two.

bacon and brune mussels

ingredients

2 Tbsp (30 mL)	butter
1/4 cup (60 mL)	bacon, cut horizontally into strips about 1/4 inch by 1 inch (0.5 by 2.5 cm)
1/4 cup (60 mL)	julienned leek
2 tsp (10 mL)	chopped garlic
2 lbs (900 g)	mussels
1/2 cup (125 mL)	Belgian dubbel (robust)
2 Tbsp (30 mL)	grainy Dijon mustard
	salt, to taste

serves 2–4

serve with: smoky or satisfying

If anyone were to ask which mussel recipe best represents beerbistro, we would have to say it was this one, which incorporates not just beer but also our in-house brined and smoked bacon. (You can make your own bacon at home—see page 174.) We're proud of all our food, but somehow the mere mention of our bacon always starts chests puffing and heads swelling in our kitchen. In this dish, the smokiness of the bacon, nutty sweetness of the beer, and gentle tang of the mustard, really enhance the flavour of the mussels.

- Heat a shallow sauté pan until very hot. Melt butter and sauté bacon, leeks, and garlic until soft and fragrant, approximately 1 minute. Add cleaned mussels and give a good shake.
- Add beer, give another shake, cover, and steam mussels for 3 minutes or until mussels just start to open.
- Add grainy mustard, give another shake, and let boil with the cover off to reduce your sauce, approximately 1 minute. Discard any shells that do not open fully during cooking. Taste and season with salt, if needed.
- Serve immediately in one large or four individual warmed bowls and pour almost all the liquid over the mussels, watching for and avoiding the grit that may sit in the last spoonful or two.

helles and herb mussels

serve with: sociable

The simple flavours of tomato and tarragon are the classic base of this Provençal-style dish, recreated with beer instead of wine. These flavours also happen to meld marvellously with the crispness of a helles-style German lager, creating a sauce that is not only great on its own but also a good base for inventive additions like other herbs, mustard, or whatever suits your fancy.

- In a shallow sauté pan over high heat, melt butter and sauté onion and garlic until soft and fragrant, approximately 1 minute. Add cleaned mussels and give a good shake. Cook for 30 seconds.
- Add beer and tomato sauce, give another shake, cover, and steam mussels for 3 minutes or until mussels just start to open.
- Add diced tomatoes and tarragon, give another shake, and let boil with the cover off to reduce sauce, approximately 1 minute. Discard any shells that do not open fully during cooking. Taste and season with salt, if needed.
- Serve immediately in one large or four individual warmed bowls and pour almost all the liquid over the mussels, watching for and avoiding the grit that may sit in the last spoonful or two.

ingredients

2 Tbsp (30 mL)	butter
1/3 cup (75 mL)	red onion, thinly sliced
2 tsp (10 mL)	chopped garlic
2 pounds (900 g)	mussels
6 Tbsp (90 mL)	helles lager (crisp)
2 Tbsp (30 mL)	tomato sauce
1/4 cup (60 mL)	diced plum tomatoes
2 tsp (10 mL)	chopped fresh tarragon
pinch	salt

serves 2–4

blue-blonde mussels

ingredients

2 Tbsp (30 mL)	butter
1/4 cup (60 g)	julienned leeks
4 tsp (20 mL)	chopped garlic
2 pounds (900 g)	mussels
6 Tbsp (90 mL)	spicy Belgian blonde ale (spicy)
1/4 cup (60 mL)	finely diced peeled pears
1/4 cup (60 mL)	mild blue cheese (such as ermite, Maytag blue, or roquefort), crumbled
2 oz (60 g)	baby spinach
pinch	salt

serves 2–4

serve with: satisfying or spicy

This dish was created as a playful riff on the pear, blue cheese, and walnut salads that have become so popular in recent years. The spiciness of the beer, the bold earthiness of the cheese, and the sweet flavours from the mussels, pears, and spinach all come together in perfect harmony.

- In a shallow sauté pan heated over high heat, melt butter and sauté leeks and garlic until soft and fragrant, approximately 1 minute. Add cleaned mussels and give a good shake.
- Add beer and diced pears, give another shake, cover, and steam mussels for 3 minutes or until mussels just start to open.
- Add blue cheese and baby spinach, give another shake, and let boil with the cover off to reduce sauce, approximately 1 minute. Discard any shells that do not open fully during cooking. Taste and season with salt, if needed.
- Serve immediately in one large or four individual warmed bowls and pour almost all the liquid over the mussels, watching for and avoiding the grit that may sit in the last spoonful or two.

monk's temptation mussels

serve with: robust or contemplative

When developing some Belgian-themed dishes for a promotion we were having at beerbistro, we thought for a bit about the things we think of as Belgian—monks, chocolate, mussels, and of course beer. This recipe, which started out as a bit of a joke but wound up wowing everyone in the kitchen, is the result. Don't dare miss out on the sauce in this one!

- In a shallow sauté pan heated until very hot, melt butter and sauté garlic, shallots, and chipotles until soft and fragrant, approximately 1 minute. Add cleaned mussels and give the pan a good shake to coat the mussels in the shallots, peppers, and garlic.
- Add beer, cover, and steam mussels for 3 minutes or until mussels just start to open.
- Remove the cover, give the pan another good shake, and let boil with the cover off to reduce sauce, approximately 1 minute.
- Add chopped parsley and chocolate and toss until chocolate is melted and dissolved into liquid, approximately 20 seconds. Discard any shells that do not open fully during cooking. Taste and season with salt, if needed.
- Serve immediately in one large or four individual warmed bowls and pour almost all the liquid over the mussels, watching for and avoiding the grit that may sit in the last spoonful or two.

ingredients

2 Tbsp (30 mL)	butter
1 tsp (5 mL)	minced garlic
3 Tbsp (45 mL)	diced shallots
2 Tbsp (30 mL)	chopped chipotle peppers
2 pounds (900 g)	mussels
1/3 cup (75 mL)	Rochefort 8 Ale (or other abbey-style robust ale)
1 Tbsp (15 mL)	chopped fresh flat-leaf parsley
1 Tbsp (15 mL)	chopped semi-sweet chocolate
pinch	salt

serves 2–4

petit déjeuner mussels

ingredients

2 Tbsp (30 mL)	butter
2 tsp (10 mL)	chopped garlic
1/4 cup (60 mL)	cherry tomatoes, halved and roasted (see sidebar below)
2 pounds (900 g)	mussels
6 Tbsp (90 mL)	oatmeal stout (satisfying)
2 Tbsp (60 mL)	tomato sauce
1/4 cup (60 mL)	watercress trimmed
3 Tbsp (45 mL)	finely chopped (chiffonade) fresh basil
pinch	salt,
1/4 cup (60 mL)	crumbled goat cheese

serves 2–4

Roasting Tomatoes

To roast cherry tomatoes, cut each one in half, season with salt and pepper, and place in a 375°F (180°C) oven until they just start to release their juices, about 7–10 minutes. Remove from the oven, let cool, and refrigerate until ready to use.

serve with: satisfying or smoky

The joke of this dish—*petit déjeuner* is "breakfast" in French—stems from the use of oatmeal stout. There's nothing funny about the taste, though, as the creamy richness of the malty stout balances the sweetness of the tomatoes, the peppery character of the watercress, and of course the dry appeal of the cheese. Remember that the cheese will melt, so if you want to enjoy little chunks of cheese in your mussels, be sure to add it at the last possible moment.

- In a shallow sauté pan heated until very hot, melt butter and sauté garlic and tomatoes until soft and fragrant, approximately 1 minute. Add cleaned mussels and give a good shake.
- Add beer and tomato sauce, give another shake, cover, and steam mussels for 3 minutes or until mussels just start to open.
- Add watercress and basil, give another shake, and let boil with the cover off to reduce sauce, approximately 1 minute. Discard any shells that do not open fully during cooking. Taste and season with salt, if needed.
- Serve immediately in one large or four individual warmed bowls, and pour almost all the liquid over the mussels, watching for and avoiding the grit that may sit in the last spoonful or two. Top with crumbled goat cheese just before serving.

weissbier–smoked salmon mussels

serve with: satisfying

This is a lovely light mussel dish with beautiful, delicate flavours. The trick is to add the smoked salmon at the very last minute so you don't cook it or make it mushy. Just allow the heat of the mussels to warm it gently at the very end.

- In a shallow sauté pan heated until very hot, melt butter and sauté garlic, fennel, and leeks until soft and fragrant, approximately 1 minute. Add cleaned mussels and give the pan a good shake to coat the mussels.
- Add beer and cream, toss again, then cover and steam mussels for 3 minutes or until mussels just start to open.
- Add parsley, give the pan another good shake, and let boil with the cover off to reduce sauce, about 1 minute. Discard any shells that do not open fully during cooking. Taste and season with salt, if needed.
- Serve immediately in one large or four individual warmed bowls, and pour almost all the liquid over the mussels, watching for and avoiding the grit that may sit in the last spoonful or two. Top with smoked salmon pieces.

ingredients

2 Tbsp (30 mL)	butter
2 tsp (10 mL)	chopped garlic
2 Tbsp (30 mL)	sliced fennel
3 Tbsp (45 mL)	chopped leeks
2 pounds (900 g)	mussels
1/3 cup (75 mL)	weissbier (quenching)
1/4 cup (60 mL)	whipping (35%) cream
2 Tbsp (30 mL)	chopped fresh flat-leaf parsley
pinch	salt
3 1/2 oz (100 g)	smoked salmon, sliced into small pieces

serves 2–4

devil's lobster club mussels

ingredients

2 Tbsp (30 mL)	butter
2 tsp (10 mL)	chopped garlic
1/4 cup (60 mL)	sliced leeks
1/4 cup (60 mL)	bacon, cut horizontally into thin strips
2 pounds (900 g)	mussels
	juice of 1/2 lemon
3 oz (90 mL)	Vienna lager (sociable)
3 Tbsp (45 mL)	whipping (35%) cream
1/2 cup (125 mL)	diced plum tomato
1 Tbsp (15 mL)	chopped fresh basil
3 1/2 oz (100 g)	lobster meat, in chunks
pinch	salt

equipment

Shallow sauté pan with a lid

Serving bowls

serves 2–4

serve with: sociable or satisfying

When we describe anything on the menu as "club," it seems to sell like wildfire, and these mussels are no exception—something about the combination of bacon and tomato, we guess! Canned lobster will work fine in this recipe, but for the best results, steam or boil a 1¼- to 1½-pound lobster and save as much as possible of the juices when you cut it apart and add them in with the meat.

- In a shallow sauté pan heated until very hot, melt butter and sauté garlic, leeks, and bacon until soft and fragrant, approximately 1 minute. Add cleaned mussels and give a good shake.
- Add lemon juice to pan, then beer and cream, give another shake, cover, and steam mussels for 3 minutes or until mussels just start to open.
- Top mussels with diced tomatoes and basil, give another shake, and let boil with the cover off to reduce sauce, approximately 1 minute. Discard any shells that do not open fully during cooking. Taste and season with salt, if needed.
- Serve immediately in one large or four individual warmed bowls, top with lobster meat (and reserved liquid, if available) and pour over almost all the liquid from the pan, watching for and avoiding the grit that may sit in the last spoonful or two.

Baked Mussels

Baked mussels are incredibly popular in Belgium—where they even have special serving trays for them—but are virtually unknown everywhere else. Maybe this is why we love these simple, easy-to-make dishes as much as our customers do.

For home dinner parties, baked mussels are a show-stopper and easy on the host, since they can be prepared ahead of time, even the day before, and simply popped into the oven at the last minute. As with steamed mussels, be sure to have plenty of good bread at hand for sopping up the delicious sauces left behind.

For all the following recipes, simply follow the steps that follow to prepare the mussels for baking.

- In a large, heavy-bottomed sauté pan over high heat, melt butter and sauté chopped garlic and shallots and any other ingredients until soft and fragrant, approximately 1 minute. Add as many cleaned mussels as you will be serving, plus several extras in case some don't open. (Allow for at least a dozen mussels per person as an appetizer.) Shake the pan until all the mussels are well coated in the butter mixture.

- Add beer, cover, and steam the mussels until they open, approximately 3 minutes. Discard any shells that do not open fully during cooking.

- Once the mussels are all open, strain off and reserve the cooking liquid, and place the mussels in the fridge to cool.

- When the mussels are cool enough to handle, gently break open the shell, remove the mussel, and replace it on one half of the shell. Arrange the mussels on the half-shell on pie plates—or Belgian mussel trays, if you can get them—and follow the rest of the recipe.

bacon, goat cheese, and arugula
baked mussels

ingredients for steaming

2 Tbsp (30 mL)	butter
2 tsp (10 mL)	finely chopped garlic
1/4 cup (60 mL)	finely diced shallots
2 pounds (900 g)	mussels (or as many as needed)
3/4 cup (175 mL)	gueuze (appetizing)

ingredients for baking

1 Tbsp (15 mL)	butter
1 Tbsp (15 mL)	garlic, chopped
4 1/2 cups (1.125 L)	arugula, finely chopped
pinch	salt and freshly ground black pepper
1/2 cup (125 mL)	garlic butter
1 cup (250 mL)	shredded mozzarella
1/2 cup (125 mL)	goat cheese, crumbled
1 cup (250 mL)	diced sautéed bacon

serves 2–4

serve with: crisp or bold

- Preheat oven to 350°F (180°C).
- Steam mussels as described on page 140.
- In a large, heavy-bottomed sauté pan over high heat, melt butter and sauté garlic until soft and fragrant, approximately 1 minute. Add arugula and cook until wilted, approximately 2 minutes. Season with salt and pepper, remove from heat, and set aside.
- To serve individually, build on pie plates; otherwise, bake on a baking sheet. Arrange half of the empty mussel shells open side upward. Place 1 tsp (5 mL) arugula mixture in the bottom of each mussel shell, then place the mussel back in the shell. Top each mussel with a 1/2 tsp (2 mL) of garlic butter, pour reserved liquid onto them, and sprinkle cheeses and bacon liberally over all the mussels.
- Bake until cheese is melted and liquid is bubbling, approximately 5–7 minutes.

garlic and cheese-baked mussels

serve with: crisp or bold

- Preheat oven to 350°F (180°C).
- Steam mussels as described on page 140.
- In a large, heavy-bottomed sauté pan over high heat, melt butter and sauté garlic until soft and fragrant, approximately 1 minute. Add spinach and cook until wilted, approximately 2 minutes. Season with salt and pepper, remove from heat, and set aside.
- To serve individually, build on pie plates; otherwise, bake on a baking sheet. Arrange half of the empty mussel shells open side upward. Place 1 tsp (5 mL) spinach mixture in the bottom of each mussel shell and then place mussel back in the shell. Top each mussel with 1/2 tsp (2 mL) garlic butter, pour the reserved liquid onto them, and sprinkle cheeses liberally over all the mussels.
- Bake until cheese is melted and liquid is bubbling, approximately 5–7 minutes.

ingredients for steaming

3 Tbsp (45 mL)	butter
3 Tbsp (45 mL)	chopped garlic
1/4 cup (60 mL)	diced shallots
2 lbs (1 kg)	mussels
3/4 cup (175 mL)	Belgian white beer (quenching)
	juice of 1/2 lemon

ingredients for baking

1 Tbsp (15 mL)	butter
1 tsp (5 mL)	chopped garlic
4 cups (1 L)	spinach, finely chopped
pinch	salt and freshly ground black pepper
1/2 cup (125 mL)	garlic butter
1 cup (250 mL)	shredded mozzarella
1/4 cup (60 mL)	shredded Parmesan cheese

serves 2–4

mushroom baked mussels

ingredients for steaming

2 Tbsp (30 mL)	butter
1 Tbsp (15 mL)	chopped garlic
1/4 cup (60 mL)	diced shallots
1/4 cup (60 mL)	finely diced leeks
1 Tbsp (15 mL)	chopped fresh thyme leaves, stems discarded
2 pounds (900 g)	mussels
3/4 cup (175 mL)	porter (satisfying)

ingredients for baking

1/2 cup (125 mL)	garlic butter
1/2 cup (125 mL)	shredded mozzarella
1 Tbsp (15 mL)	butter
1 tsp (5 mL)	chopped garlic
2 cups (500 mL)	sliced oyster and cremini mushrooms
pinch	salt and freshly ground black pepper
	juice of 1/2 lemon
1/2 cup (60 mL)	diced blue cheese

serves 2 – 4

serve with: satisfying

- Preheat oven to 350°F (180°C).
- Steam mussels as described on page 140.
- In a large, heavy-bottomed sauté pan over high heat, melt butter and sauté garlic until soft and fragrant, approximately 1 minute. Add mushrooms and cook until soft, approximately 1 minute. Season with salt and pepper, remove from heat, and set aside.
- To serve individually, build on pie plates; otherwise, bake on a baking sheet. Arrange half of the empty mussel shells, open side upward. Place 1 tsp (5 mL) mushroom mixture in the bottom of each mussel shell and then place mussel back in the shell. Top each mussel with 1/2 tsp (2 mL) garlic butter, pour reserved liquid onto them, and sprinkle cheeses liberally over all the mussels.
- Bake until cheese is melted and liquid is bubbling, approximately 5–7 minutes.

baked pizza mussels

serve with: sociable

- Preheat oven to 350°F (180°C).
- Steam mussels as described on page 140.
- To serve individually, build on pie plates; otherwise, bake on a baking sheet. Arrange half of the empty mussel shells, open side upward. Spoon the tomato sauce, oregano, and basil on top of the mussel shells. Replace mussel and top each one with 1/2 tsp (2 mL) garlic butter, pour reserved liquid onto them, and sprinkle the cheese and pepperoni liberally over all the mussels.
- Bake until cheese is melted and liquid is bubbling, approximately 5-7 minutes.

ingredients for steaming

2 Tbsp (30 mL)	olive oil
2 Tbsp (30 mL)	chopped garlic
1/2 cup (125 mL)	diced shallots
1/4 cup (60 mL)	finely diced yellow and red bell peppers
1/2 cup (125 mL)	diced plum tomatoes
2 pounds (900 g)	mussels
3/4 cup (175 mL)	Vienna lager (sociable)

ingredients for baking

1 1/2 cups (375 mL)	tomato sauce
2 tsp (10 mL)	chopped fresh oregano
1 Tbsp (15 mL)	finely shredded fresh basil
1/2 cup (125 mL)	garlic butter
1 cup (250 mL)	mozzarella, shredded
1/2 cup (125 mL)	pepperoni slices

serves 2-4

beerbistro's belgian-style frites

serve with: crisp

We think our frites are great; our customers think they're amazing! And who are we to disagree?

Really, though, we take our frites very seriously, going through a relatively simple but lengthy process to produce the best fried potatoes possible. It's a fair amount of work, but we think it's worth it, and if you follow all the steps below, we're betting you will too.

To begin, potato selection is vital to the quality of the final frites. For best results, use a potato that is rich full-bodied, and also has a low sugar content, such as russets, which we use at beerbistro. Another of our favourites is the Yukon gold for its terrific flavour.

Next, the size of the cut will determine the quality of your frites: too thin and they'll break up in the fryer and go cold quickly; too thick and they won't cook properly to the core. We use a "chipper" that cuts to a specific size, but you probably don't have one of those at home, so use a long, sharp knife and try to cut as evenly as possible, aiming for about 1/2 inch (1 cm to 1.5 cm) square.

Once cut, your frites need to soak to wash away starches and sugars that will cause the outside of the frites to overcook when the inside is still underdone. Immerse them in cold water and soak until the water clears, which should take about 15 minutes. Then drain and pat them dry, preparing them for the two-stage fry.

The two fryings are key to crisp, quality frites, as the first fry will cook the potato and the second will give it a golden crispness. Set your fryer for 300°F (150°C), and when the oil is hot, fill the basket no more than two-thirds full and fry until the frites are blanched. This should take about 3 to 4 minutes.

When they're blanched, lift the basket from the oil and let it drain for a minute before turning the frites onto baking trays to cool. The faster they cool, the better they're going to turn out, so try to spread them out as much as possible. The frites must be cool before the second fry but should never be left for more than 4 hours before refrying.

When you're ready to eat, reset your fryer to 360°F (182°C) and fry for about 4 to 5 minutes, until the frites are crisp and golden brown on the outside and tender in the middle. Drain in the basket

and then on parchment paper, and salt your frites while they're still hot and glistening.

Serve with your favourite ketchup or homemade Mayonnaise (recipe, page 207).

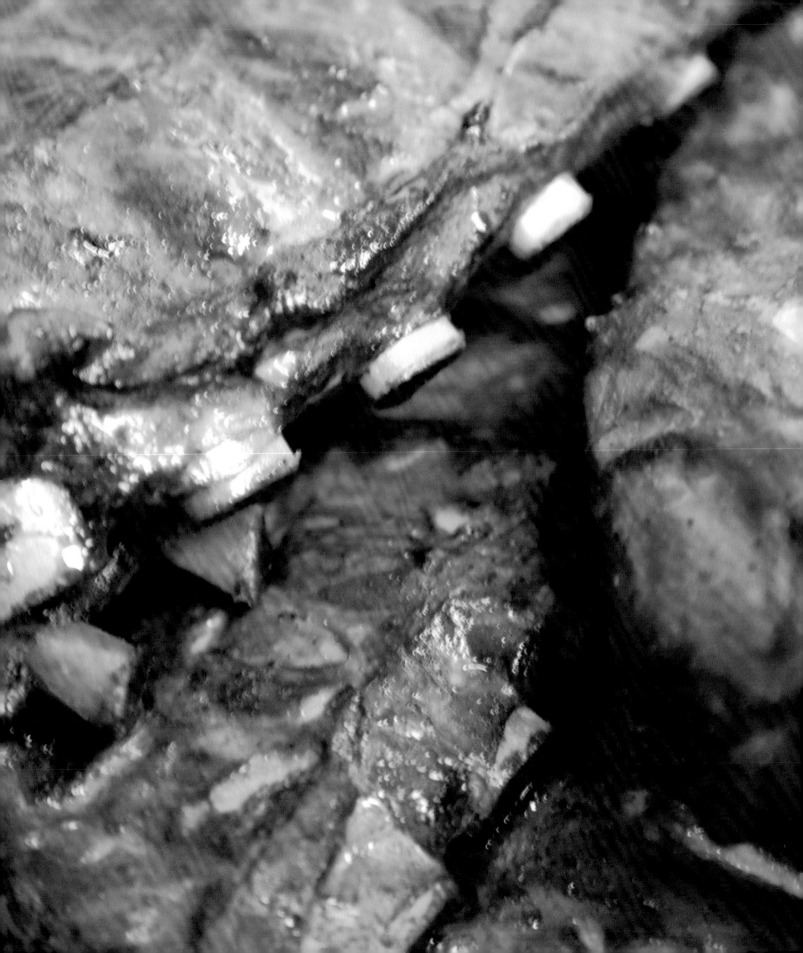

from the grill and the barbeque

There is pretty much no kind of cooking more closely associated with beer than grilling, even if it most often has more to do with what's in the chef's glass than what goes into the food! But as much as we enjoy grilling with a beer in hand—and believe us, we do!—we also love the flavours that beer can bring out in barbequed foods, from the caramelized maltiness of a true beer burger to the unbeatable moistness of a beer-brined chicken.

apple ale back ribs

ingredients

8 whole racks	baby back ribs
1 1/2	lemons, cut into wedges (about 8–10 wedges per lemon)
2 tsp (10 mL)	freshly cracked black pepper
2–3 bottles (12 oz/ 341 mL)	apple ale
2 cups (500 mL)	barbeque sauce

special equipment
Barbeque or grill (optional)

serves 8

serve with: sociable, bold, or smoky

Extra-slow cooking is the key to excellent ribs. They stay tender and juicy but never dry, and the beer braise provides additional flavour and tenderness. Be sure to allow the ribs to cool to room temperature before grilling or they can fall apart on the fire, and be careful not to burn the sauce once you do have them on the grill—the goal is to dry out the sauce just enough that it becomes sticky.

- Preheat oven to 300°F (150°C).
- Peel membrane from the underside of each rack of ribs.
- In a large roasting pan, arrange ribs so the first layer curves up from the pan, the next curves down toward the pan, and so on. This will allow for space between ribs, which is essential for proper cooking. Scatter lemon wedges and cracked black pepper over ribs. Add beer until the ribs are covered.
- Cover roasting pan with a lid or tightly cover first with plastic wrap and then with aluminum foil. Bake for 3 1/2 hours.
- After cooking time has elapsed, test ribs by inserting a fork between two centre ribs and twisting. If ribs come apart easily, test one or two other racks to make sure all the meat is evenly cooked. If ribs do not separate easily, return pan, covered, to the oven and cook for another 15 minutes before checking again. Continue until ribs are "fall off the bone" tender.
- When ribs are done, remove from oven and let cool in the beer for about an hour.

- Once ribs are cool to the touch, remove from broth and brush with barbeque sauce. Let cool. Ribs may now be covered in plastic wrap and refrigerated for later use or reheated and served immediately.
- To reheat ribs, preheat a barbeque grill to medium heat or an oven to 400°F (200°C). Grill or bake ribs until they are hot to the touch and the sauce is sticky.

lamb burgers
with stout and rosemary

serve with: crisp, bold, or robust

Believe it or not, the secret to these burgers lies in the use of bread crumbs, which absorb the stout and other liquids and keep the patties incredibly moist and juicy. Just be careful not to press down on the burgers when grilling them, or you can undo all this flavourful goodness by literally squishing out the moisture.

- Make fresh bread crumbs by breaking slices of bread into 3 or 4 pieces and processing in a blender or food processor until fine.
- Pour bread crumbs into a large stainless-steel or non-reactive mixing bowl and add all the other ingredients, mixing well until evenly incorporated.
- Cover the bowl and let sit overnight in the refrigerator to allow meat to absorb beer and other flavours.
- When ready to cook, divide meat mixture into 6 oz (175 g) balls and form each into a patty roughly 1 inch (2.5 cm) thick. Patties will seem a little soft but will firm up nicely on the grill.
- Preheat barbeque grill.
- When it is hot, brush the grill with a little oil. Place burgers on the grill and allow to cook just more than halfway through before turning them, roughly 3–4 minutes on a medium-hot grill. Flip each burger and finish cooking. For best results, flip each burger only once and never, ever flatten it onto the grill.
- Serve immediately on toasted Buttermilk-Beer Buns or other burger buns and top with sliced tomatoes, sautéed mushrooms, roasted onions, and good-quality blue or goat cheese.

ingredients

2	slices good-quality white bread
2 1/4 lbs (1.125 kg)	lean ground lamb (regular grind)
1 cup (250 mL)	stout
1	egg
1/4	medium Spanish onion, finely diced
2	cloves garlic, finely minced
2 Tbsp (30 mL)	Dijon mustard
2 Tbsp (30 mL)	ketchup
1 Tbsp (15 mL)	chopped fresh rosemary
1 Tbsp (15 mL)	chopped fresh basil
2 Tbsp (30 mL)	chopped fresh flat-leaf parsley
1 tsp (5 mL)	red hot sauce
1/4 tsp (1 mL)	Worcestershire sauce
2 tsp (10 mL)	salt
1/2 tsp (2 mL)	freshly ground black pepper
	oil
	Buttermilk-Beer Buns (recipe, page 243)
	sliced tomatoes
	sautéed mushrooms
	roasted onions
	good-quality blue or goat cheese

special equipment

Blender or food processor

Stainless-steel or non-reactive mixing bowl

Barbeque or grill

serves 8

grilled white beer salmon wrap

ingredients

2 cups (500 mL)	Hot Smoked Salmon, flaked (recipe, page 172)
1/2 cup (125 mL)	Mayonnaise (recipe page 207)
1 1/2 Tbsp (22 mL)	Dijon mustard
1	bunch green onions, chopped
1	red onion, finely chopped
2–3	lemons, zested and juiced
3 Tbsp (45 mL)	capers, finely chopped
pinch	salt and freshly ground black pepper
2 cups (500 mL)	arugula
1/2 cup (125 mL)	finely sliced red onion
1 cup (250 mL)	pea shoots
4	12-inch (30 cm) flour tortillas

serves 4 for lunch or 8 as appetizers

serve with: quenching or contemplative

The popularity of wraps doesn't appear to be waning, nor should it when there are taste treats like these still to be enjoyed! These wraps are perfect for when you're having a few people over for lunch, since they can be made and refrigerated ahead of time. Cut smaller, they are also terrific appetizers.

- Follow directions to make Hot Smoked Salmon (page 172).
- In a large mixing bowl, mix salmon, mayonnaise, mustard, green and red onions, lemon zest and juice, and capers. Combine well, seasoning with salt and pepper if needed.
- Divide arugula, shaved onion, and pea shoots evenly between 4 tortillas, arranging ingredients in a wide line down the middle. Top each tortilla with one-quarter of the salmon salad. Roll the sides over and press lightly but firmly so the wrap won't come apart.
- Roll each wrap in plastic wrap or aluminum foil and store in the refrigerator until needed or cook immediately on a hot grill until grill lines appear, roughly 1 minute.
- Slice in half and serve immediately for a light meal, or cut in eighths to serve as appetizers.

grilled lamb loin niçoise

ingredients

18 oz (500 g)	lamb loin
pinch	salt and freshly ground black pepper
3	quail eggs, hard-boiled and halved
4 oz (110 g)	green beans, blanched
4 oz (110 g)	cherry tomatoes, yellow and red mixed, halved
1/4 cup (60 mL)	caperberries, halved
1/4 cup (60 mL)	black olives, pitted and halved
4 oz (110 g)	mini red potatoes, boiled and quartered
1/4 cup (60 mL)	Tarragon and Ale Vinaigrette (recipe, page 203)

special equipment

Stainless-steel or non-reactive mixing bowl

Barbeque or grill

serves 2

serve with: contemplative

For some reason, summer salads always seem to be either vegetarian or seafood. However, we love this grilled lamb variation on the classic niçoise salad, and we bet you will too!

- Preheat the barbeque to medium-high.
- Season lamb loin generously with salt and pepper.
- Grill loin until rare, turning it on the grill to produce cross-hatch grill marks. Remove lamb from grill and let sit for 1 minute before cutting in half on a bias.
- Divide all remaining ingredients except lamb, potatoes, and vinaigrette between two plates.
- In a stainless-steel or non-reactive mixing bowl, toss potatoes with 2 Tbsp (30 mL) vinaigrette and arrange evenly around the perimeter of the plates.
- Top each salad with half of the loin and drizzle with remaining vinaigrette.

roasted knuckle of pork
marinated in dopplebock

serve with: crisp or contemplative

Admittedly, the very idea of pork knuckles still bothers some people, but removing the meat from the bone cuts down considerably on the ick factor, and the combination of sweet, slow-roasted meat and salty brine, plus malty doppelbock, is sure to make a convert of even the most squeamish carnivore.

- In a large bowl, combine all ingredients except knuckles and water. Stir.
- Add pork knuckles and enough water to ensure that meat is completely submerged. Cover and refrigerate for 24 to 36 hours.
- Preheat oven to 275°F (140°C).
- Remove knuckles from brine and place on a roasting rack. Roast for 6 hours or until the bone twists easily out of the meat.
- Using a sharp paring knife or kitchen shears, snip and remove the crackling (skin). Separate meat from bone and divide evenly between four plates. Top each portion of meat with some crackling.

ingredients

1	meduim cooking onion, sliced
2	cloves garlic, sliced
2 cups (500 mL)	dopplebock (contemplative)
4 1/2 cups (1.25 L)	cider vinegar
5	sprigs fresh rosemary, leaves removed and stems discarded
5	sprigs fresh thyme, leaves removed and stems discarded
2	pork knuckles (pork hocks)
	water, as needed

special equipment

Roasting rack

Sharp paring knife or kitchen shears

serves 4

spice-rubbed oatmeal stout chicken

ingredients

4 lb (2 kg)	roasting chicken
1 1/2 cups (375 mL)	oatmeal stout (satisfying)
3 Tbsp (45 mL)	kosher salt
1/4 cup (60 mL)	lightly packed brown sugar
1/4 cup (60 mL)	sliced shallots
1 Tbsp (15 mL)	Worcestershire sauce
2	cloves garlic, sliced
2 tsp (10 mL)	green hot sauce
2 Tbsp (30 mL)	red hot sauce
1 Tbsp (15 mL)	Dijon mustard
1 Tbsp (15 mL)	chopped fresh tarragon
1 Tbsp (15 mL)	chopped fresh rosemary
3 Tbsp (45 mL)	Chicken Spice Rub (see sidebar, page 165)

special equipment

Strong knife or kitchen shears

Tongs

Barbeque or grill

serves 4

serve with: crisp or sociable

Brining is a great way to keep chicken moist and tender, even when served cold a day or two later, and the oatmeal stout in this brine creates a flavour that's simply outstanding. Don't be concerned if there is a thin layer of pink next to the skin of your bird after cooking—that's not raw chicken but the flavourful smoke ring!

- Prepare chicken by rinsing it well inside and out with cold water and patting dry with paper towel. Next, using a strong knife or kitchen shears, remove any excess fat from the cavities and cut off the wing tips. Stand bird up so the hind cavity is on top facing up and run your knife down the backbone to cut chicken in half. Remove the backbone and save along with the wing tips to use later in stock.
- In a deep medium bowl, stir together beer, brown sugar, and salt until dissolved. Add remaining ingredients and mix well. Submerge chicken in brine and cover. Refrigerate for 24 hours.
- Remove chicken from brine, pat dry with paper towels, and rub thoroughly with Chicken Spice Rub. Let rest for 1 hour.
- Preheat the barbeque to a low heat, approximately 225°F (110°C).
- Place chicken halves, skin side down, on the grill and close barbecue lid. Cook until skin is golden brown and crispy. Turn the pieces and continue cooking until the internal temperature of the bird reaches 160°F (72°C). Cut each half into 4 pieces and serve.

chicken spice rub

2 Tbsp (30 mL)	cumin seeds
1 Tbsp (15 mL)	ground coriander
1 Tbsp (15 mL)	hot pepper flakes
1 Tbsp (15 mL)	fennel seeds
1 Tbsp (15 mL)	whole cloves
2 Tbsp + 2 tsp (40 mL)	juniper berries
2 Tbsp (30 mL)	Hungarian (sweet) paprika
1/3 cup (75 mL)	chili powder
1 Tbsp (15 mL)	ground cinnamon
1/4 cup (60 mL)	pickling salt

- Combine all the ingredients and mix well.
- Store in a sealed jar in the cupboard for up to 4 months.

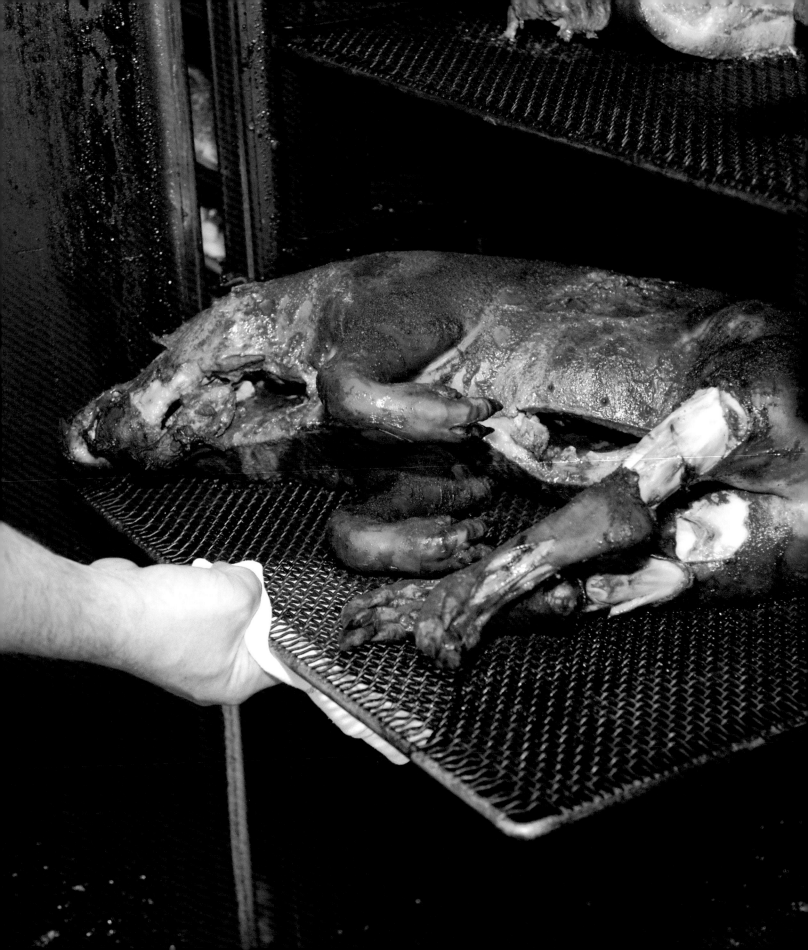

the butcher shop

There's something incredibly satisfying about making your own sausages or curing your own gravlax, and it's a feeling that's even better when there is beer involved! These recipes create some of the most popular items at beerbistro.

duck confit

ingredients

8	duck legs
1/4 cup (60 mL)	Duck Confit Cure (2 tsp for each leg) (see sidebar, page 169)
3–4 lb (1.5–2 kg)	rendered fat

rendering duck fat

I find this is the best way to render fat.

- Place whatever fat you have in a large pot, completely cover it with water, bring to a boil, then reduce the heat and simmer for a couple of hours, taking off any scum that rises to the top of the pot.
- Strain into a tall container, and place in the fridge until the fat has congealed. Remove the fat from the container, discarding the water, and it's ready to use. Fat stays fresh in the freezer for quite a long time.

serve with: contemplative or robust

Confit means "to preserve" and is a classic style of cooking in French bistros. The technique of confit is to submerge different meats, fish, shellfish, or vegetables in fat and slow cook. As for fat, duck or goose are the best, but pork fat, or lard, can also be used. We regularly confit duck, rabbit, pork bellies, and garlic at the bistro. Confit of salmon or lobster are also pretty amazing, using butter as the fat. So many different tastes and textures can be achieved from a confit, depending on the length of time the ingredient is in the cure and how slowly you cook it.

- Trim any excess fat off duck legs. Score the skin around the bone just under the drumstick knuckle so skin can shrink while cooking and reveal the bone nicely.
- Cure legs on the exposed meat side; place legs, skin side down, in a container, and chill, covered, for 24 hours.
- Preheat the oven to 310°F (155°C).
- Lightly rinse off Duck Confit Cure under cold water.
- Place the legs in a deep ovenproof dish or braising pan and cover with melted fat. Cover and cook for 2–2 1/2 hours. To check to see if legs are done, remove a leg from the fat and push the skin side. When you feel the meat giving away from the bone, remove from the oven and leave to cool in the fat.
- When cool, remove the legs from the fat and place in a clean dish and cover with the fat. This will keep, chilled, for a long time.

Duck Confit Cure

- Mix all ingredients together, place in a clean Mason jar or other container, and refrigerate. This cure has a shelf life of 1 month.

ingredients

1/4 cup (60 mL)	chopped fresh flat-leaf parsley
1/2 Tbsp (7 mL)	freshly ground black pepper
1 Tbsp (15 mL)	chopped fresh thyme
1/2 Tbsp (7 mL)	orange zest
1/2 tsp (2 mL)	lime zest
1/2 tsp (2 mL)	lemon zest
1 1/2 cups (375 mL)	kosher salt
1/2 cup (125 mL)	granulated sugar

makes 2 1/3 cups (600 mL)

wild boar sausage

ingredients

2 slices	good-quality white bread
4 lbs (2 kg)	wild boar shoulder (should be about 25%–28% fat)
6 oz (180 g)	roasted garlic and shallots
5	branches fresh rosemary, finely chopped
1 Tbsp (15 mL)	juniper berries, cracked
2 tsp (10 mL)	freshly cracked black pepper
2 Tbsp (30 mL)	yellow mustard seeds, toasted
1 oz (30 g)	salt
2/3 cup (150 mL)	Belgian-style spiced ale (spicy)
	natural casings

special equipment

Blender or food processor

Meat grinder

Sausage stuffer

makes 16–20 large sausages

serve with: quenching, especially dunkelweissbier, in the morning; sociable in the afternoon

One of the great things about these sausages is that, because of the incredible flavour the garlic and shallots bring to them, they are lower in fat than many similar links. We recommend using natural lamb sausage casings if you're making them to fry or grill on their own and hog casings if you're planning to use them for pizza or mussels.

- Make bread crumbs by breaking slices of bread into 3 or 4 pieces and processing in a blender or food processor until fine.
- With a very sharp knife, cut boar shoulder into about a 1-inch (2.5 cm) dice and combine with other ingredients in a large bowl. Cover and marinate in the refrigerator for at least 3 hours.
- Put the mixture through a meat grinder with a fine blade into a chilled bowl. As an alternative, take the mixture to your local butcher shop and ask them to grind it for you. Stir the mixture well to incorporate all the ingredients.
- Use a little of the meat to form a small patty and fry it at medium heat so you can taste the sausage. Adjust seasoning in the remaining uncooked meat if necessary and chill it in the refrigerator for 2–4 hours.
- Stuff into natural casings using a sausage stuffer. Refridgerate until ready to use.

white beer–cured salmon

serve with: quenching or satisfying

Whether simply cured or smoked, our salmon is not only incredibly popular with our customers, but also amazingly versatile as a dish unto itself or an ingredient in everything from salads to wraps. For a wonderful hors d'oeuvre to serve at your next party, place a little cured salmon on coin-sized Porter Pancakes (recipe, page 199) and top with Sweet Mustard Sauce (recipe, page 209) and a little chopped red onion.

- In a large, shallow roasting pan just big enough to hold the salmon, place fish, skin side down, and cover completely with the Salmon Cure, making sure to distribute it evenly. Cover and place the pan in the refrigerator for 12 hours.
- Remove from the refrigerator and gently pour beer over fish, taking care not to wash off crust. Cure for a further 24–36 hours in the fridge.
- Remove salmon from beer and rinse off the cure. Pat dry and slice thinly to serve or wrap in plastic wrap and return to refrigerator for up to a week.

ingredients

4 lb (2 kg)	side Atlantic salmon
16 oz (450 g)	Salmon Cure (see sidebar)
4 1/4 cups (1.125 L)	Belgian-style white beer (quenching)

serves 15

salmon cure

ingredients

7 oz (210 g)	coarse salt
9 oz (250 g)	granulated sugar
1 tsp (5 mL)	ground coriander
	zest of 1 orange

- In a bowl, mix together all ingredients. Use immediately or store in a sealed jar in the refrigerator for up to 1 month.

Smoking Salmon, Hot and Cold

There are two ways to smoke salmon: at a very low temperature over a long period of time (cold smoking) or at a high temperature for a shorter time (hot smoking). Apart from the different flavours each method brings to the fish, the main difference is that cold smoking preserves the fish, while hot smoking actually cooks it.

In terms of flavour, cold smoking tends to yield a taste that's similar to what you'll buy at the store, while hot smoking produces a more intense, almost oily smokiness. The textures will be different too: cold-smoked salmon is firm, with the same consistency as cured salmon only lightly smoky, and hot-smoked salmon resembles grilled or baked salmon.

At beerbistro, we hot and cold smoke as needed, something we're able to do thanks to some highly specialized equipment. For home cooking, however, hot smoking is really the best way to go, since it is not only easy to do with a home smoker or barbeque, but also produces salmon that is ready to eat a lot faster.

For hot smoking, you'll first need to choose a wood to use in either your barbeque or smoker. We prefer fruit wood, specifically apple wood, but really any hard wood will do. Use whatever is your favourite.

If using a smoker, build your fire as directed in the unit's instructions. For a gas barbeque, soak the wood chips in water first, then put them in a bowl made out of heavy-duty aluminum foil and place on one side of the preheated grill. For a charcoal barbeque, place the chips directly on top of a smouldering fire built on one side of the grill.

Add salmon to the smoker or place on the side of the barbeque without flame and close the cover. Try to maintain a relatively low heat of under 160°F (72°C) for the first 2 hours so the fish will absorb as much smoke as possible, then increase the temperature to roughly 212°F (102°C), and cook until a thermometer inserted into the middle of the fish reads 165°F (75°C). At this point, salmon should be flaky and moist but will no longer appear wet.

Serve immediately or store wrapped in the refrigerator for up to 6 days for later use.

beer-cured pork belly
(or, you too can make your own bacon)

ingredients

3 cups (750 mL)	cold water
1 1/2 cups (375 mL)	kosher salt
1 cup (250 mL)	lightly packed brown sugar
1 tsp (5 mL)	black peppercorns
5	juniper berries
2	cloves garlic, crushed
3	sprigs fresh thyme, leaves removed and stems discarded
6 cups (1.5 L)	malty, fruity beer (robust or soothing or fruity)
2	sides pork belly

special equipment

Very large pan or bowl

Smoker or barbeque

serve with: smoky

When our kitchen staff chat with first-time beerbistro customers at our chef's table, it's never long before the conversation turns to our bacon. Definitely a huge favourite with our regulars, this is even more popular in the kitchen, as it's one of the unique things we do that really sets beerbistro apart. The key of course is the beer, which needs to be fruity and malty, never hoppy, to contribute the kind of richness and flavour that truly sets beerbistro bacon apart from the rest.

- In a large saucepan over medium-high heat, bring water, salt, brown sugar, peppercorns, juniper berries, garlic, and thyme to a boil. Continue boiling until salt and sugar are dissolved.
- Remove from the heat and let the mixture steep for 20 minutes.
- Strain liquid and transfer to a very large pan or bowl. Stir in cold beer and refrigerate.
- When brine has completely cooled, add pork bellies, cover them completely with the brine, and refrigerate for about a week.
- Preheat a smoker or barbeque to 300°F (150°C)
- Place bellies in the smoker for 30 minutes. Reduce the heat to 185°F (85°C) and continue to smoke for 4 hours.
- Remove bellies from the smoker and allow to cool.
- Return bellies to the smoker, rebuild the fire to 225°F (110°C), and smoke for a further 3 hours.
- Slice and use as needed. Store remainder in refrigerator, covered, for up to 3 weeks or freeze.

porter-braised pulled pork

serve with: smoky or bold

Sure you could say this is a big recipe and takes a while to finish, but that would be to ignore the fact that it's so versatile, being great on its own, in a sandwich, or as a topping for everything from pizza to pasta, and freezing extremely well. In fact, once you make this tender, moist, tasty pork for the first time, we're betting you'll want to make it a regular habit.

- Preheat smoker or barbeque to roughly 200°F (100°C). Add wood chips either directly to smoker or in an aluminum foil bowl on the side of barbecue without flame.
- Rub pork all over with Barbecue Spice. Place pork in smoker or on the side of the barbecue grill without flame, fat side up over a drip tray. Smoke for 6–6 1/2 hours.
- Preheat oven to 225°F (110°C).
- Remove pork from the smoker or grill and transfer to a roasting pan, add 2 1/2 cups beer, cover, and place in oven for 4–6 hours or until meat pulls apart easily with a fork.
- Remove pork from pan and shred with a fork so that it resembles strings, removing any connective tissue or bones.
- Place pork in a large, heavy-bottomed saucepan and add barbeque sauce, malt vinegar, and remaining beer. Simmer until liquid is mostly evaporated and the meat is moist but not sloppy.
- Use immediately or store, well wrapped, in the refrigerator for up to 8 days, or freeze for up to 3 months.

ingredients

1	pork shoulder (2– 3 lbs/1–1· kg)
1/4 cup (60 mL)	Barbeque Spice Rub (recipe, page 100, or use your favour-ite brand)
3 cups (750 mL)	porter, divided
2 cups (500 mL)	barbeque sauce
1/2 cup (125 mL)	malt vinegar

special equipment

Smoker or barbeque

Wood chips, preferably apple or other fruit wood

serves 8 as a main course

beer and cheese

9

orget all that talk you've heard about wine and cheese. The real partner for everything from cheddar to stilton is beer. But don't take our word for it—ask a sommelier! Any honest wine professional will admit that the motto in the grape trade is "taste with bread, sell with cheese," primarily because the fats in cheese will help blot out the tannins and other harsh notes that may show up in youthful or aggressive wines.

Beer and cheese, on the other hand, well, that's just a match made in gastronomic heaven. The trick, as ever, is simply picking the right style of beer for each particular kind of cheese.

One classic wine that complements a cheese is port and stilton, since the sweetness of the wine will soften and round the sharp edges of that great cheese and other blues like it, such as French roquefort, American Maytag blue, and Québécois ermite. The cheese, however, does no great favours for the port. This is why we prefer a strong and sweet, but slightly bitter, ale like a good barleywine. For the most powerful veined blue cheeses, such as Spanish cabrales, hoppy Imperial stout pairs well as it provides some resistance to the bite of the cheese and makes the match more a partnership of equals.

Milder cheeses like cheddars still benefit from a little sweet fruitiness in the beer, but also need less alcohol and hoppiness to balance the partnership, which is why we take our cue from the pub classic, the ploughman's lunch, and pair cheddar and similar cheeses with off-dry, nutty, or mildly fruity but still moderately hoppy beers like that other icon of the pub, best bitter. Dry and nutty brown ales also fare well in this pairing, as does the malty British style of pale ale, but it's best to save citrusy American-style pale ales and IPAs for only the oldest and sharpest of cheddars.

Another nation that provides us with a cue for beer and cheese pairing is Belgium, since most of that country's beers are strong and malty and the majority of its cheeses mild and pungent. Okay, let's not mince words: most Belgian cheeses stink but are surprisingly soft in both texture and taste, qualities that make them ideal partners for the strongly malty and aromatic ales that Belgium is best known for. The sweet and sometimes spicy nose of such beers tempers the olfactory assault of the cheese, the fruitiness of the beer harmonizes with similar characteristics in the cheese, and the oiliness of the alcohol enhances even further the cheese's creamy appeal, all without dousing the poor cheese in bitterness. The wedding here, be it raw milk brie de Meaux from France and Belgian abbey ale or a rich and ripe camembert and strong North American spiced ale, is between like-minded attributes, and a happy and flavourful marriage it is indeed.

For the remaining types of cheese, from nutty, aged gouda to soft and sensuous havarti, the trick is to look for beers of similar qualities, being sure never to overwhelm the taste of the cheese with high-powered bitterness. So pair that gouda with an equally dry and nutty brown ale, that havarti with a gentle and fruity blonde ale, and a young and delicately flavoured goat cheese with a Belgian-style wheat beer. Further on in the taste scale, try a not-too-hoppy helles lager for an older and drier chèvre; a sweet, strong, and rounded doppelbock for a smelly but not terribly fruity or forceful limburger; a well-cellared and mellowed American-style barleywine for an equally aged and robustly flavourful Parmigiano Reggiano and . . . well, we're sure you get the point by now.

So put away your corkscrews and break out the beer the next time cheese is on the menu. You may get a curious sideways glance from the wine snobs in the crowd, but everyone else will likely enjoy themselves immeasurably more. And for accompaniment, try one of the tasty relishes that come next.

cheese type	examples	beer characteristics	examples	the ultimate pairing
Soft, moist, mild flavour, goat milk	Almost any North American-made cheese labelled "chèvre" or "soft goat cheese"	Light body, spicy and/or lightly fruity	Belgian or German wheat beer; light, blonde ale; helles	A Belgian-style wheat with a balanced expression of orange and coriander
Semi-soft, dry, goat milk, some sharpness of taste	Chabichou du Poitou; Crotin de Chavignol	Moderate hoppiness, crisp flavour, dry finish; alternately, tart and very dry	Bohemian Pilsner; hoppier versions of Kölsch; bière de garde; saison; traditional gueuze	One of the few instances where a well-made, moderately hoppy continental Pilsner will shine
"Bloomy" rind, some funkiness of flavour (especially when raw milk), mild sharpness	Camembert; brie de Meaux; Edam; havarti; morbier	Drying rather than bittering hop, toasty or roasty malt profile, very dry finish	Stout; porter; altbier; brown ale; some drier versions of Belgian dubbel	A rich and creamy oatmeal stout
Semi-soft, mild character, fruity flavour	Epoisses de Bourgogne; Livarot; Chimay à la bière	Moderately sweet character, minimum hop influence, caramel or fruity flavours	Bock; Irish ale; Scottish ale; Belgian enkel and some dubbels	A balanced, not-too-sweet bock would be a beautiful thing
Washed rind, strong and pungent aroma, soft interior, fruity	Aged cheddar; gruyère; Ossau-Iraty; manchego	Strong flavours, spicy, higher than average strength, lingering finish	Strong spiced ales in the Belgian style; British-style barleywines; strong abbey ales	Even if you don't believe that "quadruppel" is a legitimate style, and we don't, anything labelled as such would be lovely
Firm texture, sharp and fruity-nutty flavours, lingering aftertaste	Parmigiano Reggiano; aged gouda; Old Amsterdam	Moderate to high hoppiness, balancing malt, dry character	British-style pale ale; best bitter; some dunkels (for milder cheeses); dry stouts	An English farmhouse cheddar and a pint of good best bitter will please almost anyone
Hard texture, grainy, crumbly, nutty and sharp flavours	Cambozola; Cashel Blue; Stilton	Firm maltiness, little apparent hop bitterness; dry but creamy character; roast or smokiness optional	Irish ales; nutty brown ales; malt-dominated porters; rauchbiers	A bourbon barrel-aged porter or strong brown ale
Mild to moderately sharp and creamy, blue veined, milky taste	Roquefort; Cabrales; gorgonzola	Sweet, malty character, some strength and notable alcoholic warmth, nutty to roasty malts	Sweet stouts; strong dubbels; doppelbocks; British-style barleywines	Old-school British barleywines can have alcohol contents as low as 7% or 8%, which would suit these cheeses to a tee
Sharp, blue veined, aggressive, mouth drying		Big alcohol, big body, formidable hop presence but always balanced with maltiness, long finish	"Double" IPAs; American-style barleywines; very strong Belgian-style ales	Some American barleywines tend forcefully toward the hoppy side, but one with a little restraint would be welcome here

belgian spiced ale onion confit

ingredients

1 Tbsp (15 mL)	duck fat (or vegetable oil)
10	Vidalia or other sweet onions, sliced
1 cup (250 mL)	Belgian or Belgian-style spiced ale (spicy)
1 cup (250 mL)	cider vinegar

makes 4 cups (1 L)

A big batch of this confit will never go to waste, as it's as great an accompaniment to cheese as it is to pâtés or terrines, or even as a garnish for beautifully grilled steak.

- In a medium saucepan over medium heat, heat duck fat or oil. Stir in onions.
- Reduce heat to medium-low, cover, and cook onions until deeply golden and very soft, about 4 hours.
- Increase heat to medium, add the beer and vinegar, and continue to cook until texture becomes thick and jammy, about 30 minutes.
- Store in the refrigerator in a sealed jar for up to 3 months. Allow to warm to room temperature before using.

rodenbach and plum compote

When fresh plums appear in the fall, that's the time to make a big batch of this ideal accompaniment for a wide variety of cheeses, from soft and stinky to aged and nutty. For variety's sake, you can make a batch with cherries, or even apricots or peaches, instead of the plums.

- In a deep stainless-steel or other non-reactive pot over medium heat, reduce beer until it becomes syrupy.
- Add plums and cook until they are just heated through and the skins begin to release their colour.
- Transfer plums and liquid to Mason jars and seal immediately.
- Working in batches, if necessary, place jars in a large pot of boiling water and process for 30–45 minutes.
- When properly processed, these will keep for 6 months. Once opened, keep refrigerated for up to 7 days.

ingredients

24 oz (710 mL)	Flemish sour red ale (appetizing)
2 1/2 lbs (1.2 kg)	Italian prune plums, each pitted and chopped into 8 equal pieces

special equipment

Deep stainless-steel or other non-reactive pot

8–12 (8 oz/250 mL) Mason jars

Large pot

makes 8–12 (8 oz/250 mL) jars

the pantry

From great ingredients come even greater dishes! This section contains all the little extras that our customers tell us make dining at beerbistro so special, from our signature chocolate stout jelly to a pair of wonderful, barbeque-friendly slaws.

brown ale chili

ingredients

1 Tbsp (15 mL)	oil
2 1/4 lbs (1 kg)	ground beef
2	medium sweet onions, finely diced
6	cloves fresh garlic, chopped
5 Tbsp (75 mL)	Mexican chili spice
2 Tbsp (30 mL)	dried thyme
2 Tbsp (30 mL)	ground cumin
1 cup (250 mL)	drained rinsed canned kidney beans
2 1/2 cups (625 mL)	brown ale (sociable)
1 can (28 oz/796 mL)	chunky tomato sauce
1 tsp (5 mL)	red hot sauce
	salt

makes about 8 1/2 cups (2 L)

Great on its own with a loaf of bread and served with a sociable, bold or spicy beer or to spice up Nachos (recipe, page 96) or tacos.

- In a heavy-bottomed saucepan over high heat, heat oil. Add ground beef, broken up so it fries evenly. Cook until browned, remove from heat, and drain off and discard fat.
- Return beef to heat and add onions and garlic. Cook until onions are softened and garlic is lightly cooked and fragrant.
- Add spices and stir meat so it is well coated. Stir in kidney beans, beer, and tomato sauce. Mix well and simmer, covered, for 1 1/2–2 hours or until thick and bubbly.
- Add hot sauce and salt if needed. Serve immediately or cover and refrigerate for up to 5 days.

gueuze sour cream dumplings

We use these light and delicious dumplings in our Coq au Bier (recipe, page 114), but they are equally tasty in any hearty soup or braised dish.

- In a large mixing bowl, mix together flour, baking powder, parsley, and salt and set aside.
- Meanwhile, place softened butter, beer, and Gueuze Sour Cream in a medium saucepan over low heat and gently warm it to roughly body temperature, making sure not to bring to a boil.
- Slowly add beer mixture to flour mixture, kneading or mixing with a fork until it just comes together. Be careful not to overmix, as this will cause dumplings to become tough.
- Pull off 3 Tbsp (45 mL) pieces and gently roll each into a ball.
- Bring a saucepan of vegetable or chicken stock (or water) to a boil and simmer dumplings for 5–8 minutes, being careful not to overcook.

ingredients

2 cups (500 mL)	all-purpose flour
1 Tbsp (15 mL)	baking powder
2 Tbsp (30 mL)	finely chopped fresh flat-leaf parsley
1 tsp (5 mL)	kosher salt
2 Tbsp (30 mL)	butter, softened
2 Tbsp (30 mL)	Belgian-style white beer (quenching)
3/4 cup (175 mL)	Gueuze Sour Cream (recipe, page 194), unwhipped
	chicken or vegetable stock or water

makes 24 dumplings

gueuze sour cream

ingredients

4 1/2 cups (1.125L)	whipping (35%) cream
1/3 cup (75ml)	gueuze
1 Tbsp (15ml)	yogurt

This is a wonderfully flavourful sour cream. The gueuze gives it a beautiful sour fruity freshness, and the little bit of yogurt adds to that citrusy tartness. The great thing about this sour cream is that you can use as is or you can whip it up and make it lighter and more delicate.

- In a medium stainless-steel saucepan on medium heat, heat cream until it's lukewarm, about 100°F (38°C), then add gueuze and yogurt.
- Remove from heat and cool uncovered to room temperature.
- Cover and let sit out at room temperature overnight for at least 24 hours or until the mixture thickens. Refridgerate and use as needed.
- If you are close to running out, make more by mixing 1 cup (250 mL) of gueuze sour cream and 4 cups (1L) of whipping (35%) cream and heat until it's lukewarm. Leave it out to cool then refrigerate.

mustard seed spaetzle

We serve these wonderful little dumplings with our Kriek-Braised Rabbit (recipe, page 116), but they fare equally well with pork or chicken dishes. For a change of pace, mix them with cheese sauce for a creative take on classic mac and cheese.

- In a bowl, combine all ingredients and thoroughly mix dough until smooth. Let dough rest for 1 hour to relax the gluten.
- To cook, press dough through a spaetzle press into boiling water or spread it on a board and cut into small strips about 1–2 inches (2.5–5 cm) long, then drop a handful at a time into the boiling water.
- Once spaetzle float to the surface of the water, remove them with a slotted spoon or small sieve and set aside to cool on a tray, brushing them lightly with oil to prevent sticking. To reheat, plunge spaetzle in hot water or fry quickly in a pan.

ingredients

2 cups (500 mL)	all-purpose flour
1/3 cup (75 mL)	whole milk
3/4 cup (175 mL)	Belgian-style white beer (quenching)
2	eggs
1/2 cup (125 mL)	sour cream
1 Tbsp (15 mL)	yellow mustard seeds, toasted gently in a frying pan and cracked
	salt and freshly ground black pepper, to taste

makes 8–10 servings

banana-onion jam

ingredients

1 Tbsp (15 mL)	light vegetable oil
2–3	white onions, thinly sliced
1	ripe banana, finely chopped
1 cup (250 mL)	granulated sugar
1 cup (250mL)	cider vinegar
1 cup (250 mL)	malty Belgian-style ale (robust)

makes 1 1/4 cups (300 mL)

This flavourful chutney is a great accompaniment to pâtés, cured meats, or cheeses.

- In a small stainless-steel saucepan over low heat, heat oil. Add onions and slowly cook, covered, until they caramelize, about 2 hours.
- Preheat oven to 350°F (180°C).
- Sterilize clean Mason jars by placing them in oven for 15 minutes. Sterilize lids by boiling them in water for 15 minutes. New lids are best.
- Reduce heat to medium-high and add banana, gently stirring until the banana softens and starts to dissolve. Add sugar and cook until the sugar begins to caramelize, being careful not to burn the mixture.
- Slowly add vinegar, stirring constantly. Reduce heat to medium and stir in beer. Reduce the mixture until a "jammy" consistency is reached.
- Transfer jam to sterilized jars with tight-fitting lids and seal. Place the jars in a pot of boiling water and boil for 20 minutes to preserve.
- Cool and store in the fridge. Keeps for 6 months.

chocolate-stout jelly

This is an excellent accompaniment to the Chicken Liver–Foie Gras Mousse (recipe page, 82).

- Place the gelatin leaves in bowl of cold water for 5–7 minutes or until soft.
- Meanwhile, in a heavy-bottomed saucepan, bring stout almost but not quite to a boil. Add cocoa and sugar and whisk to remove any lumps. Bring mixture to a boil.
- Remove from heat and strain through fine strainer into a shallow bowl.
- While liquid is still hot, stir in gelatin, then place in refrigerator to cool. The mixture will set to a jelly-like consistency.
- Refridgerate in an airtight container for up to 10 days.

ingredients

3	gelatin leaves
1/2 cup (125 mL)	oatmeal stout (satisfying)
1/4 cup (60 mL)	unsweetened cocoa powder
1 1/2 Tbsp (20 mL)	granulated sugar

makes 2/3 cup (150 mL)

tomato-avocado salsa

ingredients

4	Roma tomatoes, seeded and diced
1/2	red onion, finely diced
2	avocados, diced
4	green onions, chopped
	juice of 2 limes
1 tsp (2 mL)	finely chopped garlic
1/4	bunch fresh coriander, finely chopped
pinch	salt and freshly ground black pepper, to taste

makes 2 1/2 cups (625 mL)

We use this tasty salsa as an accompaniment for our popular Lobster Quesadilla (recipe, page 109), but it's just as good with a bowl of tortilla chips.

- Mix all ingredients together in a serving bowl and season to taste with salt and pepper.
- Serve immediately or cover and refrigerate for up to 2 days.

roasted pineapple raita

We offer this as a condiment for our Blonde Ale Pakoras (recipe, page 87) but find it can be used as a fine addition to almost any type of curry or even as a simple vegetable dip. Do note, however, that although this is a simple recipe, it does call for a day's preparation beforehand.

- The night before making raita, drain yogurt by wrapping it in cheesecloth and placing it in a strainer suspended over a bowl. Refrigerate overnight, discarding any liquid.
- The next day, preheat the oven to 375°F (190°C).
- Peel and cut pineapple into pieces roughly 1 inch (2.5 cm) square and roast until cooked and a little caramelized on the sides, approximately 15 minutes. Remove from the oven and let cool.
- In a food processer, blend cooled pineapple with drained yogurt and cumin. Taste and season with salt as needed. Store in the refrigerator in an airtight container for up to 5 days.

ingredients

2 cups (500 mL)	yogurt
1/4	pineapple
1 tsp (5 mL)	ground cumin
1 tsp (5 mL)	salt

special equipment

Cheesecloth

Food processor

makes about 2 cups (500 mL)

porter pancakes

ingredients

1 1/2 cups (375 mL)	all-purpose flour
2 tsp (10 mL)	baking powder
1 tsp (5 mL)	salt
1 1/2 cups (375 mL)	porter (satisfying)
4	eggs
1/4 cup (60 mL)	butter, melted and cooled
5–6 drops	red hot sauce
1/2 tsp (2 mL)	Worcestershire sauce

makes 24 pancakes, 1 1/2 inch (4 cm)

Our customers love these little blini-like pancakes with our White Beer–Cured Salmon (recipe, page 171).

- In a large mixing bowl, combine flour, baking powder, and salt.
- In a separate mixing bowl, whisk together porter, eggs, and melted butter.
- Working slowly, mix flour mixture into porter mixture, being careful not to let lumps form. Stir in hot sauce and Worcestershire sauce and allow to rest in the fridge for 1 hour before using.
- In a hot frying pan over medium heat, drop 1 Tbsp (15 mL) batter for each pancake and cook until bubbles form on tops and pancakes seem firm. Flip pancakes and cook the other sides until lightly brown.

lemon, white beer,
and truffle vinaigrette

This is an essential ingredient in the Apple-Fennel Slaw (recipe, page 209) and also a fine dressing for the Bistro Salad (recipe, page 79) or any other green salad. Mixed with grilled onions, it also makes a delicious topping for beef tacos.

- Place shallots, garlic, mustard, lemon juice, vinegar, beer, salt, and pepper in a large mixing bowl. With a hand-held blender or whisk, slowly whisk in oils, mixing constantly to emulsify. When mixture is fully integrated, stir in parsley and Worcestershire sauce and reseason to taste.
- Store in sealed container in fridge for up to 8 days.

ingredients

1/4 cup (60 mL)	finely chopped shallots
1/2 Tbsp (7 mL)	finely chopped garlic
1 Tbsp (15 mL)	Dijon mustard
2 Tbsp (30 mL)	freshly squeezed lemon juice
1 cup (250 mL)	cider vinegar
1/4 cup (60 mL)	Belgian white beer (quenching)
1/2 tsp (2 mL)	salt, or to taste
1/4 tsp (1 mL)	freshly ground black pepper, or to taste
2 cups (500 mL)	vegetable oil
1/4 cup (60 mL)	truffle oil
1 Tbsp (15 mL)	chopped fresh flat-leaf parsley
1/4 tsp (1 mL)	Worcestershire sauce

makes approximately 4 cups (1 L)

pink grapefruit and
pickled ginger vinaigrette

ingredients

1	ruby red grapefruit
1/2 tsp (2 mL)	dry mustard
1 tsp (5 mL)	Dijon mustard
1 Tbsp (15 mL)	freshly ground pink peppercorns
1 1/2 Tbsp (22 mL)	pickled ginger
1/4 cup (60 mL)	red wine vinegar
1 Tbsp (15 mL)	liquid honey
1 1/2 cups (375 mL)	canola oil

makes 2 cups (500 mL)

This light and zesty dressing is a great addition to cold seafood dishes, such as our Cured Salmon Salad (recipe, page 80).

- Segment grapefruit over a bowl to catch all the juice. Reserve the segments for another use.
- Place all ingredients except oil into a deep bowl. Using a hand-held blender or whisk, slowly drizzle oil in until it is completely incorporated and dressing is fully emulsified.
- Store in sealed container in fridge for up to 6 days.

tarragon and ale vinaigrette

- In a mixing bowl, combine egg yolks, mustard, vinegar, and beer.
- While whisking or using hand blender, drizzle oil into mixture to form an emulsion.
- Add tarragon and mix thoroughly. Season with salt and pepper as needed.

ingredients

2	egg yolks
1 Tbsp (15 mL)	Dijon mustard
1 cup (250 mL)	tarragon vinegar (tarragon steeped in red wine vinegar)
1/2 cup (125 mL)	weissbier
3 cups (750 mL)	olive oil
1 bunch	fresh tarragon, leaves removed and stems discarded
pinch	salt and freshly ground pepper

white beer butter sauce

ingredients

1 cup (250 mL)	cider vinegar
1/2 cup (125 mL)	Belgian-style white beer (quenching)
4	black peppercorns, freshly ground
1/2 tsp (2 mL)	kosher salt
1	sprig fresh thyme, leaves removed and stems discarded
1/2	clove garlic, crushed
2	shallots, sliced
1 Tbsp (15 mL)	whipping (35%) cream
1 cup (250 mL)	unsalted butter, cubed

makes 1 cup (250 mL)

At beerbistro, we've used this sauce for our White Beer–Poached Salmon (recipe, page 117) but also find it works brilliantly on most fish or even as a simple pasta sauce.

- In a medium stainless-steel saucepan over medium heat, combine vinegar, beer, pepper, salt, thyme, garlic, and shallots and bring to a simmer. Reduce mixture until syrupy.
- Add cream and reduce again until just a glaze.
- Remove pan from heat and whisk in butter, piece by piece, until fully incorporated and emulsified.
- Strain through a fine strainer and return to pan to keep warm. Use immediately.

mayonnaise

A good homemade mayo is a must for beerbistro's Belgian-Style Frites (recipe, page 150).

- In a large mixing bowl, whisk together egg yolks, mustard, salt, and vinegar until just foamy. Continuing to whisk, slowly pour oil into egg mixture, working slowly so the oil can be incorporated into eggs.
- Once all oil has been added and mayonnaise is fully emulsified, it should be thick enough to dip a French fry but not snap it in half. Adjust the consistency with very hot water, if needed. Season to taste with Worcestershire and hot sauce.
- Best enjoyed immediately, but can be stored in the refrigerator in an airtight container for up to 8 days.

ingredients

6	egg yolks
1/3 cup (75 mL)	Dijon mustard
1/2 tsp (5 mL)	salt
1/4 cup (60 mL)	cider vinegar
3 cups (750 mL)	vegetable oil
6 drops	Worcestershire sauce
3 drops	red hot sauce

makes about 4 1/2 cups (1.125 L)

great coleslaw

dressing

2 cups (500 mL)	Mayonnaise (recipe page 207)
	juice of 1 lemon
	juice of 2 limes
1/4	large onion, finely grated
1 Tbsp (15 mL)	finely minced garlic
1 Tbsp (15 mL)	brown sugar
1 tsp (5 mL)	celery salt
1 Tbsp (15 mL)	kosher salt
1/2 Tbsp (7 mL)	freshly ground black pepper
3/4 cup (175 mL)	cider vinegar

coleslaw base

1/2	head cabbage, thinly shredded
1/4	red bell pepper, thinly sliced
1/4	yellow bell pepper, thinly sliced
1/2	red onion, thinly sliced
1/4	bulb fennel, thinly sliced
1/2	bunch green onions, thinly sliced
1/2	bunch fresh flat-leaf parsley, chopped

makes 3 cups (750 mL) dressing and enough slaw to serve 10–12

A great coleslaw is a must when serving great barbeque ribs. There's something about the acidity of the lemon, lime, and vinegar that cuts through the smoke and the fat of the meat and refreshes your palate. To make this for a crowd, shred all your ingredients ahead of time, even a day or two prior, then toss them with the dressing an hour or two before serving, so the flavours have time to blend, and then again right before serving, so the slaw is nice and moist. For a variation, add 2 chopped hard-boiled eggs and 1 cup (250 mL) cooked sliced snow peas at the end.

- *To make the dressing:* In a large mixing bowl, whisk together Mayonnaise and lemon and lime juice. Stir in onion, garlic, brown sugar, celery salk, salt, and pepper. Whisk in cider vinegar until smooth.

- *To make the salad:* In a large serving bowl, toss all slaw ingredients until well mixed. Add the dressing and toss again until all slaw is well coated.

apple-fennel slaw

A fine accompaniment to smoked ribs, pulled pork, or almost anything barbequed.

• Place all ingredients in a large bowl and toss with vinaigrette and vinegar. Taste and season with salt and pepper.

1	bulb fennel, finely sliced
1/4	head savoy cabbage, finely sliced
2	green apples, peeled and grated or julienned
1	bunch chives or green onions, finely chopped
1/2 cup (125 mL)	Lemon, White Beer, and Truffle Vinaigrette (recipe, page 201)
1/2 cup (125 mL)	cider vinegar
pinch	salt and freshly ground black pepper, to taste

serves 8

oatmeal stout balsamic glaze

ingredients

2 cups (500 mL)	oatmeal stout (satisfying)
2 cups (500 mL)	balsamic vinegar
1 cup (250 mL)	turbinado or other raw granu-lated sugar

makes about 1 cup (250 mL)

Talk about versatile! This glaze can be used to complement vegetables, salads, chicken, or salmon, not to mention other firm-fleshed fish. And best of all, it will keep almost indefinitely in the refrigerator, but we're betting it will be completely enjoyed long before that becomes an issue.

- In a stainless-steel saucepan over medium heat, combine stout, beer, and sugar and reduce until sauce is thick and coats the back of a spoon.
- Store in an airtight container in the refrigerator for as long as you want.

sweet mustard sauce

We serve this tasty sauce with our White Beer–Cured Salmon (recipe, page 171), but it's also great on sandwiches or with a tasting tray of cold cuts or cured meats.

- In a mixing bowl, whisk together lemon juice and dry mustard powder until dissolved. Whisk in Dijon mustard, sugar, and egg yolk until combined.
- Still whisking, slowly drizzle in oil until fully incorporated and emulsified. Add dill and adjust seasonings if necessary.
- Store in a sealed container in the fridge for up to 10 days.

ingredients

	juice of 1/4 lemon
1 tsp (5 mL)	dry mustard
2 Tbsp (30 mL)	Dijon mustard
1 tsp (5 mL)	granulated sugar
1	egg yolk
1/2 cup (125 mL)	vegetable oil
2 Tbsp (30 mL)	chopped fresh dill

makes about 1 cup (250 mL)

11

the pastry shop

Beer for dessert? Well, just like beer is not just for bar-rooms and pool halls anymore, there's no need to limit your beer cuisine to the main parts of your meal. In fact, many beer styles, particularly those born in or inspired by Belgian breweries, blend so well with chocolate and other dessert flavours that you'll wonder why it took you so long to try them!

chocolate success cake
with barleywine

ingredients

12 oz (350 g)	semisweet chocolate
1/4 cup (60 mL)	unsweetened cocoa powder
2/3 cup (125 mL)	barleywine ale (soothing)
1 cup (250 mL)	whipping (35%) cream
6	large eggs
1/2 cup (125 mL)	granulated sugar
	icing sugar

special equipment

10-inch (24 cm) Springform cake pan

serves 8–10

serve with: soothing

Chocolate and beer is a natural combination, particularly when the chocolate is rich and intense and the beer malty and rounded and, well, soothing. Choose a British-style barleywine or similar sweet, malty ale for this cake.

- Preheat oven to 325°F (160°C).
- Grease a 10-inch (24 cm) springform cake pan and dust with icing sugar.
- Melt chocolate with cocoa powder and beer in a large stainless-steel bowl placed on top of a medium saucepan filled with water on medium-low heat. Mix until smooth, remove from heat, and set aside.
- In a second large bowl, whip cream until stiff peaks begin to form, being careful not to overwhip. (If the peaks are too firm, cream will be difficult to incorporate later.)
- In a separate bowl, whip together eggs and sugar until a thick foam is achieved, approximately 4–5 minutes. Gently fold one-third of egg mixture into melted chocolate mixture until smooth. Repeat with remaining two-thirds of egg mixture. Fold in whipped cream until batter is completely blended and smooth.
- Pour batter into prepared pan (it will not be completely filled) and wrap the bottom in aluminum foil to prevent possible seepage.
- Place a large roasting pan, filled not more than halfway with water, on the middle rack of the oven and place the cake pan in the water bath. Bake for 1 hour, then reduce the temperature to 250°F (120°C) and bake for an additional 30 minutes.

- When cake is firm and a toothpick inserted comes out clean, remove pan from the oven and slide a knife around the edge of the pan. The cake will fall like a soufflé and achieve greater density. Let cake cool completely and dust with icing sugar just before serving.

beer butter tarts

ingredients

2 cups (500 mL)	lightly packed brown sugar
1 1/2 cups (375 mL)	corn syrup
1/2 cup (125 mL)	butter, softened
3/4 cup (175 mL)	Belgian or Belgian-style strong ale (soothing)
5	large eggs
1 recipe	Almond Sweet Dough (recipe, page 236)

special equipment

Food processor, or electric mixer with paddle attachment

12-cup Muffin tin

makes 8

serve with: spicy

These tarts are tasty enough on their own, or if you like, add raisins, chopped pecans, or chocolate chunks to the tarts before filling with the sugar and beer mixture.

- In a food processor, or an electric mixer fitted with the paddle attachment, combine sugar, corn syrup, and butter and beat until smooth. Add beer and eggs and continue to mix until smooth.
- Preheat oven to 325°F (160°C).
- Roll out Almond Sweet Dough, cut to fit muffin tins, and line tart shells with dough, allowing a bit to overlap at the top.
- Bake blind (with no filling) until shells turn a blonde colour, about 7–8 minutes.
- Remove tart shells and fill with prepared mixture.
- Reduce the oven temperature to 300°F (150°C) and bake for 10 to 12 minutes or until the mix has set and is not too wet.

beeramisu

serve with: contemplative

We know the name of this is a cheesy pun, but, really, how could we resist? Tiramisu remains a remarkably popular dessert, and the addition of a little coffee porter makes it that much better. For extra flavour, make this the day before you plan on serving it and refrigerate overnight.

- In a saucepan over medium-high heat, bring 2 cups (500 mL) cream and vanilla bean to a boil. Then remove from heat and let cool.
- In a large mixing bowl, whip mascarpone with remaining 1/4 cup (60 mL) cream and 1/4 cup (60 mL) sugar. Remove vanilla bean from cream and whip in remaining 1/4 cup (60 mL) sugar until soft. Fold cream into cheese.
- In a medium bowl, mix together porter and coffee.
- Dip ladyfingers, one or two at a time, into porter mixture and place them in the bottom of a 12-inch (30 cm) square serving dish or pan until the surface is completely covered. Top ladyfingers with half of cheese mixture and spread evenly. Repeat the process with ladyfingers and porter mixture until the first cheese layer is covered. Top with remaining cheese and spread until smooth and even.
- Dust top with cocoa powder and refrigerate until ready to serve.

ingredients

2 1/4 cups (560 mL)	whipping (35%) cream, divided
1	vanilla bean, split in half lengthwise
8 oz (225 g)	marscapone cheese, divided
1/2 cup (125 mL)	granulated sugar, divided
1 package of 16–20	ladyfingers
1/4 cup (60 mL)	coffee porter (satisfying)
1/4 cup (60 mL)	strong brewed coffee
	unsweetened cocoa powder

special equipment

12-inch (30 cm) Square serving dish or pan

serves 10

chocolate fondue

ingredients

2 1/2 lbs (1.2 kg)	semi- or bittersweet chocolate
1 cup (500 mL)	whipping (35%) cream
3/4 cup (175 mL)	framboise beer (fruity)

special equipment

Large, heatproof bowl or fondue pot

serves 12–16

serve with: soothing

We think that adding fruit beer keeps this light. Serve with fresh fruit, such as strawberries, chunks of pineapple or pear, orange segments, or, if you want to be truly indulgent, ladyfingers or pieces of brownie.

- Chop chocolate as finely as possible. Place in a large, heatproof bowl or fondue pot.
- In a heavy-bottomed saucepan over medium-high heat, bring cream and beer to a boil.
- Pour boiling liquid over chopped chocolate and let sit for 20 seconds. Whisk until chocolate is smooth and transfer to a fondue pot if necessary .

chocolate–peanut butter cappuccino

ingredients

3/4 cup (175 mL)	coffee porter (satisfying)
2 1/2 cups (625 mL)	whipping (35%) cream
4 oz (110 g)	semi- or bittersweet choco-late, finely chopped
11	eggs
3 1/2 oz (100 g)	granulated sugar
1 oz (30 g)	espresso or very strong coffee, brewed (optional)
1 tsp (5 mL)	vanilla extract
1 recipe	Peanut Butter Mousse (see sidebar, page 221)
	milk foam, additional whipped cream, or unsweet-ened cocoa powder

special equipment

Cappuccino cups

serves 10

serve with: robust

The people at Reeses's were right when they decided that chocolate and peanut butter taste great together, and the popularity of this dessert is testament to the fact. If you have oversized cappuccino cups, use them for serving, or substitute small bowls or coffee cups. When filling them, leave room for whipped cream or steamed milk, and always top with a little shaved chocolate or cocoa powder to complete the faux cappuccino effect.

- Preheat oven to 300°F (150°C).
- In a saucepan over medium heat, bring beer and cream to a boil. Once the mixture is boiling, whisk in chocolate until smooth.
- In a bowl, whisk together eggs and sugar until light and fluffy. Temper egg mixture by whisking in one-third of hot chocolate mixture. When mixture is smooth, whisk in remaining two-thirds chocolate mixture. Whisk in espresso and vanilla.
- Half fill cappuccino cups with chocolate mixture.
- Place a deep roasting pan on the middle rack of the oven and put the cups in it. Fill pan with hot water so the cups are surrounded with water, about halfway up. Bake until custard is no longer liquid but still has some movement, approximately 30 minutes. Remove from oven and let cool.
- When custard has completely cooled, fill cups with Peanut Butter Mousse, being sure to leave a little room at the top. Top with milk foam or whipped cream and cocoa powder.

peanut butter mousse

ingredients

4 oz (110 g)	smooth peanut butter
3 Tbsp (45 g)	icing sugar
2/3 cup (150 mL)	whipping (35%) cream

special equipment

Electric mixer

- In a large mixing bowl, combine all ingredients and beat with an electric mixer on low until combined. Switch speed to high and whip for 5 minutes or until the texture is light and airy and the colour pale brown.

beerscream

I scream, you scream, we all scream for beer ice cream.

12

beery berry sorbet

ingredients

10 oz (285 g)	frozen strawberries
3 oz (110 g)	frozen raspberries
4 oz (125 g)	granulated sugar
2 Tbsp (30 mL)	corn syrup
1 1/2 cups (375 mL)	framboise beer (fruity)

special equipment

Immersion blender

Ice cream machine

makes about 4 cups (1 L)

serve with: fruity

This sorbet is not only light and refreshing, as a good sorbet should be, but also incredibly versatile. Got some apricot beer and fresh apricots? Use them in place of the framboise and berries. Peach beer and peaches? Go for it! Blueberry beer and blueberries? Why not? Let your imagination run wild!

- In a large saucepan over medium-high heat, bring all ingredients to a boil. Using an immersion blender, mix until smooth and well combined.
- Pass through a fine strainer to remove any bits of skin or seeds.
- Process in an ice cream machine according to the manufacturer's directions.

peachy frozen yogurt

ingredients

24 oz (700 g)	peaches, peeled and stoned, or frozen
1 1/2 cups (375 mL)	peach beer (fruity)
12 oz (360 g)	granulated sugar
1/4 cup (60 mL)	corn syrup
2 1/4 (560 mL)	plain yogurt

special equipment

Blender

Ice cream machine

makes about 6 cups (1/2 L)

serve with: fruity or spicy

Although not quite a "from scratch" frozen yogurt, since we cheat a bit by not actually making the yogurt, we're betting you'll find this superior to any store-bought frozen yogurt. If you prefer, substitute any other fruit and fruit beer combination, such as apricots and apricot beer, blueberries and blueberry beer, or even a multi-fruit combination

- In a large saucepan over medium-high heat, bring peaches, beer, sugar, and corn syrup to a boil.
- Transfer to a blender and blend on high until as smooth as possible.
- Transfer to a large mixing bowl and whisk in yogurt.
- Process in an ice cream machine according to the manufacturer's directions.

pumpkin and xo ice cream

serve with: spicy

XO is a French beer that is mixed with a small amount of cognac, thus raising the alcohol content slightly. If you can't find this beer, you can come close to replicating it by adding about 1 oz (30 mL) or to taste of cognac or good brandy to 11 oz (341 mL) of relatively low-alcohol spicy beer.

- In a large mixing bowl, using an electric mixer, beat together egg yolks and granulated sugar until light and fluffy.
- In a saucepan over medium-high heat, bring cream to a boil.
- Remove from heat and, whisking constantly, slowly add cream to egg mixture. Whisk in beer.
- Return the saucepan to low heat and combine pumpkin pie filling, maple syrup, and brown sugar. Cook, stirring constantly, for 3 minutes. Add spices and cook, still stirring, for another 2 minutes.
- Remove spiced mixture from the heat and whisk into the cream mixture.
- Process in an ice cream machine according to the manufacturer's directions.

ingredients

9	egg yolks
6 oz (180 g)	granulated sugar
2 1/4 cups (560 mL)	whipping (35%) cream
11 oz (341 mL)	XO beer
1 1/4 cups (210 mL)	pumpkin pie filling
2 Tbsp (30 mL)	pure maple syrup
8 oz (450 g)	brown sugar
1 tsp (5 mL)	ground cinnamon
1/4 tsp (1 mL)	freshly grated nutmeg
1/4 tsp (1 mL)	ground ginger
1/4 tsp (1 mL)	ground cloves
1/4 tsp (1 mL)	ground allspice

special equipment

Electric mixer

Ice cream machine

makes about 4 cups (1 L)

rochefort 8, chocolate,
and chocolate chip ice cream

serve with: robust or soothing

It's long been a belief of Stephen's that Rochefort 8, the great Belgian Trappist ale, is one of the best companions chocolate could ever hope for, so when it came time to create a decadently, chocolatey ice cream, it seemed the ideal choice. You can make this with another robust ale, but we're not guaranteeing it will be as good!

- In a saucepan over medium heat, heat cream until almost but not quite boiling.
- In a large mixing bowl, whip egg yolks and sugar together until pale and fluffy.
- In a medium mixing bowl, combine chocolate and cocoa powder and pour in hot cream. Whisk until melted and smooth.
- Whisk one-third of chocolate mixture into egg mixture until smooth. Repeat with remaining chocolate. Stir in beer and combine well.
- Process in an ice cream machine according to the manufacturer's directions.
- Remove ice cream from the machine, stir in the chocolate chips, and allow to set in the freezer.

ingredients

2 2/3 cups (650 mL)	35% cream
12	egg yolks
6 oz (180 g)	granulated sugar
6 oz (180 g)	semi- or bittersweet chocolate, finely chopped
2 oz (60 g)	unsweetened cocoa powder
1 1/3 cups (325 mL)	Rochefort 8 (robust)
8 oz (225 g)	semisweet chocolate chips

special equipment

Ice cream machine

makes about 6 cups (1.5 L)

stout and skör bar ice cream

ingredients

9	egg yolks
5 oz (140 g)	granulated sugar
2 1/4 cups (560 mL)	whipping (35%) cream
1 1/4 cups (310 mL)	sweet Caribbean stout (contemplative)
12 oz (360 g)	Skör bar, chopped

special equipment

Ice cream machine

makes about 5 cups (1.25L)

serve with: robust or soothing

Our most popular ice cream! The combination of sweet stout and the caramel and chocolate of the Skör blend beautifully in this indulgent treat. If you can't get a Caribbean stout like Dragon or Royal Extra, feel free to substitute a Baltic-style porter (the Polish Okocim or Estonian Saku are good ones) or, in a pinch, a milk stout or sweet Imperial stout.

- In a large bowl, whisk together egg yolks and sugar until light and fluffy.
- In a saucepan over medium-high heat, bring cream to a boil.
- Remove from heat and, whisking constantly, slowly add cream to egg mixture. Whisk in beer.
- Process in an ice cream machine according to the manufacturer's directions.
- Remove ice cream from the machine, stir in chopped Skör bar, and allow to set in the freezer.

13

the bake shop

"Baking with Beer" might sound like the name of some sort of odd *Saturday Night Live* sketch, but really it's a great way to add moisture, rich colour, and, most important, great flavour to baked goods of all sorts. For these recipes, as with most that involve baking, we frequently use weight rather than volume measures.

stout brownies

serve with: robust or soothing

With the richness of oatmeal stout enhancing the already sensuous nature of the chocolate, these brownies are moist, gooey, and addictive, or at least that's what our customers tell us. Watch your baking time closely, though, or you risk drying them out.

- Preheat the oven to 325°F (160°C).
- Grease a 12-inch (30 cm) square cake pan.
- In the top of a double boiler over medium heat or in a bowl suspended over a pot of simmering water, melt chocolate and butter, then stir in cocoa powder. Remove from heat and, if using a double boiler, transfer chocolate mixture to a mixing bowl and let cool.
- In a separate bowl, using an electric mixer, beat eggs and sugar together until thick and fluffy. Gently fold in chocolate mixture.
- In a large mixing bowl, mix together flour, cornstarch, and salt. Add chocolate mixture to flour, mixing until well incorporated, then add beer, nuts, and chocolate chips. Stir until everything is well mixed.
- Transfer mixture to prepared pan and bake for 20–25 minutes. Make sure the centre is still a little loose to ensure the brownies remain moist.

ingredients

2 oz (60 g)	semi- or bittersweet chocolate
2/3 cup (150 mL)	unsalted butter
1 1/2 oz (45 g)	unsweetened cocoa powder
3	large eggs
8 oz (225 g)	granulated sugar
4 oz (110 g)	all-purpose flour
1/2 oz (15 g)	cornstarch
pinch	salt
1/3 cup (75 mL)	oatmeal stout (satisfying)
1/2 cup (125 mL)	macadamia nuts
1/2 cup (125 mL)	semisweet chocolate chips

special equipment

12-inch (30 cm) Square cake pan

Double boiler

makes about 24 2-inch squares

almond sweet dough

ingredients

1 cup (250 mL)	butter
5 oz (150 g)	granulated sugar
	vanilla extract, to taste
2	large eggs
13 oz (365 g)	cake and pastry flour
4 oz (110 g)	ground, blanched almonds

special equipment

Electric mixer with paddle attachment

serve with: fruity or soothing

The beauty of this dough is not just its versatility—it makes a great tart shell and can even be used on its own to create a batch of almond shortbread cookies—but also its longevity. It will stay fresh for weeks in the refrigerator or up to 6 months if well wrapped and frozen. When you want to use it, allow it to warm until it's just a little cooler than room temperature, as it becomes soft and difficult to work with if it becomes any warmer.

- In an electric mixer fitted with the paddle attachment, cream butter, sugar, and vanilla until smooth. With the mixer at medium speed, add eggs one at a time, scraping the bowl down between each addition and mixing until smooth. Add in dry ingredients and mix until just combined.
- Use immediately or wrap well in plastic wrap and refrigerate or freeze for later use.

potato-weissbier bread

serve with: sociable

This dough can also be formed into buns instead of a loaf with equally fine results. It's perfect for serving with hearty winter soups or stews.

- In an electric mixer fitted with a dough hook, on low speed, mix flour, sugar, salt, and yeast. Keeping the speed on low, mix in potatoes and butter until just combined. Mix in beer and buttermilk until combined, then turn mixer to high and mix for 7 minutes.
- Transfer dough to a lightly oiled mixing bowl and cover with a clean dish towel. Let rest in a warm place until the dough has doubled, about 2 hours.
- Punch dough down, releasing the air. Form dough into a round ball and cover again with the dish towel. Let rest for approximately 15–20 minutes.
- While dough is resting, preheat the oven to 350°F (180°C).
- Place dough in a greased or nonstick 5- by 9-inch (2 L) loaf pan, or bake free-standing on a greased or nonstick baking tray. Bake for 7 minutes, rotate pan, and continue baking for a further 5 minutes or until golden brown and a toothpick inserted into the centre of the loaf comes out clean.
- If making buns, weigh out 4 oz (110 g) dough for each bun and space them evenly apart on a greased or nonstick baking tray. Bake for 5 minutes before turning the tray around and baking for an additional 4 minutes or until the buns are golden brown and a toothpick inserted into the centre of a bun comes out clean.

ingredients

16 oz (450 g)	all-purpose flour
1 Tbsp (15 mL)	granulated sugar
1/2 Tbsp (7 mL)	salt
1 package (1/4 oz/7 g, or 2 tsp/10 mL)	active dry yeast
1/2 lb (225 g)	potato, cooked and mashed
2 Tbsp (30 mL)	butter, softened
2/3 cup (150 mL)	weissbier (quenching)
1/2 cup (125 mL)	buttermilk

special equipment
Electric mixer with a dough hook

makes 1 loaf or 10 buns

holy banana bread

ingredients

2 1/2 cups (675 mL)	cake and pastry flour
2 Tbsp (30 mL)	baking powder
1 tsp (5 mL)	ground cinnamon
1/8 tsp (0.5 mL)	freshly grated nutmeg
1/8 tsp (0.5 mL)	ground allspice
2	whole cloves, crushed
1/4 teaspoon (1 mL)	ground ginger
1 cup (250 mL)	butter, softened
2/3 cup (150 mL)	lightly packed brown sugar
2	large eggs
1 cup (250 mL)	ripe bananas, mashed (about 2)
1 cup (250 mL)	Trappist ale or similar strong Belgian-style ale (soothing)

special equipment

Electric mixer

Two 9- by 5-inch (2 L) loaf pans

make 2 loaves

serve with: robust or spicy

Because we use a Trappist abbey ale in the recipe, we joke that this moist and delicious banana bread is "holy." Serve it with any of our "beerscream" ice creams (recipes, pages 223–230).

- Preheat the oven to 325°F (160°C).
- Grease and flour two 9- by 5-inch (2 L) loaf pans.
- In a large mixing bowl, sift and mix flour, baking powder, and spices.
- In a separate mixing bowl, using an electric mixer on high speed, cream together butter and brown sugar until pale and fluffy. Still with the mixer on high, add eggs one at a time, mixing after each addition until fully incorporated and scraping down the sides of the bowl with a spatula. Using the spatula, gently fold in banana and one-third of dry ingredients. Then very gently fold in remaining dry ingredients and beer, working only until the mixture is smooth. (Overworking dough will cause the bread to come out tough and rubbery.)
- Divide batter evenly between prepared loaf pans and bake for 45 minutes or until a toothpick inserted in the centre of a loaf comes out clean.

- Remove from the oven and allow the loaves to cool in their pans for a few minutes, then turn out onto wire cooling racks and brush with glaze (see sidebar). Cool before serving.

glaze

ingredients

2 Tbsp (30 mL)	butter
2 Tbsp (30 mL)	Trappist ale or similar strong Belgian-style ale (soothing)
1 cup (250 mL)	icing sugar

- In a saucepan over medium-high heat, combine butter, beer, and icing sugar and bring to a boil. Boil for 3 1/2 minutes to reduce glaze and evaporate alcohol.
- Brush banana bread with glaze while both are still hot. If glaze cools and hardens, gently reheat until soft enough to work with.

farmhouse cheddar biscuits

ingredients

1 1/2 cups (375 mL)	all-purpose flour
1/2 cup (125 mL)	yellow cornmeal
2 Tbsp (30 mL)	granulated sugar
2 tsp (10 mL)	salt
1 1/2 Tbsp (22 mL)	baking powder
1/2 Tbsp (7 mL)	baking soda
2 cups (500 mL)	farmhouse cheddar
1/2 cup (125 mL)	cold butter
1	large egg
3/4 cup (180 mL)	buttermilk
1 bunch	green onions, sliced
2	chipotle peppers, finely chopped

special equipment

Two 12-cup muffin tins

makes 16 biscuits

serve with: bold or satisfying

In the southern United States, biscuits are an essential part of almost any meal, but especially good barbeque like our Apple Ale Back Ribs (recipe, page 156). If you wish, you can try these with jalapeños in place of chipotle peppers or omit the hot stuff completely.

- Preheat the oven to 325°F (160°C).
- Grease 16 cups of two 12-cup muffin tins.
- In a large mixing bowl, combine flour, cornmeal, sugar, salt, baking powder, and baking soda. Mix well.
- Using a grater, grate cheese and the butter into the dry ingredients. Mix together with your hands until texture becomes mealy. Add remaining ingredients and, using your hands or a wooden spoon, combine until just brought together. Do not overmix, or biscuits will become tough.
- Evenly distribute the biscuit dough in the prepared muffin tins and bake for 10 minutes. Rotate the tins and finish baking for another 5 minutes or until a toothpick inserted in the centre of a biscuit comes out clean and the tops are golden brown.

buttermilk-beer buns

serve with: sociable when topped or used for a sandwich;
bold or crisp with a burger

These tasty little gems can be topped with all sorts of ingredients,
from sliced raw onion to poppy seeds to tomato sauce and grated
cheese, just prior to baking. Plain or topped, they make great buns
for our Lamb Burgers with Stout and Rosemary (recipe, page 159) or
Porter-Braised Pulled Pork (recipe, page 177).

- In a large mixing bowl, combine flour, yeast, sugar, and salt, then
  stir in the remaining ingredients.
- Transfer to an electric mixer with a dough hook and, on low
  speed, mix until everything is incorporated. Turn speed to high
  and continue mixing for 7 minutes.
- Transfer dough to a greased mixing bowl and cover with a clean
  dish towel. Let rest in a warm place until dough has doubled,
  about 2 hours.
- Punch dough down, releasing the air, and cover again with the
  dish towel. Let rest for 15–20 minutes, until it's easy to shape into
  balls.
- Preheat oven to 350°F (180°C).
- Pull off about 4 oz (110 g) dough, form into a bun, and place on a
  greased or nonstick baking sheet. Repeat until all dough is used
  and bake for about 14 minutes or until golden brown.

ingredients

18 oz (500 g)	bread flour
2 packages	(each 1/4 oz/7 g or 2 tsp/10 mL) active dry yeast
2 Tbsp (30 g)	granulated sugar
1 Tbsp (15 g)	salt
1	extra-large egg
3/4 cup + 2 Tbsp (200 mL)	buttermilk
3/4 cup (175 mL)	beer (satisfying)
3 Tbsp (45 mL)	vegetable oil

special equipment
Electric mixer with dough hook

makes 16 buns

14

beer cocktails

Although they may sound like some new and distinctly odd drink craze, beer cocktails have a long and rich history dating from centuries-old mixtures of beer and wine; to beer blends of the sort that eventually became porter; to Colonial-era "flips" made with spirits, sometimes port wines, sugars, spices, and raw egg. The following potations are our modest contribution to this long tradition.

almondberry

ingredients

1 oz (30 mL)	amaretto
12 oz (355 mL)	sweet raspberry or cherry beer (fruity)

- Pour amaretto into a glass that will hold at least 14 oz (470 mL). Top with chilled beer and serve.

any port in a storm

Named for the impressive and intense Storm King Imperial Stout from Pennsylvania's Victory Brewing Company.

ingredients

2 oz (60 mL)	late bottle vintage (LBV) port wine
12 oz (355 mL)	Imperial stout (soothing)

- Pour port into a glass at that will hold least 16 oz (500 mL). Top with Imperial stout and serve.

belgian redhead

Inspired by Bernadette, the goddess of the back bar at Philadelphia's Monk's Café. For a Belgian Brunette, substitute a Flemish-style brown ale for the red ale.

ingredients

3/4 oz (22 mL)	vodka
3/4 oz (22 mL)	Mandarin Napoleon
11 oz (341 mL)	tart Flemish-style red ale, such as Rodenbach (appetizing)

• Pour vodka and Mandarin Napoleon into a tulip-shaped glass that will hold at least 14 oz (470 mL). Top with Rodenbach or similar Flemish-style red ale.

bière flambée

First discovered in a Paris beer bar, this method of serving strong ale is guaranteed to make an impression.

ingredients

1 1/2 oz (45 mL)	very superior old pale (VSOP) cognac
11 oz (341 mL)	strong (9% alcohol or greater) sweet ale, brought to room temperature (soothing or dark and spicy)

- Carefully heat a brandy snifter that will hold at least 14 oz (470 mL) over a boiling kettle or the steaming wand of an espresso machine until it is hot to the touch. Pour in cognac and warm it by swirling it in the glass. Carefully ignite it with a long match or wand-style lighter.
- Slowly and deliberately pour beer down the side of the glass so it creeps below the spirit, raising cognac and the flame as it goes. The flame will extinguish about two-thirds to three-quarters of the way up the glass, but the beer will continue to warm.

black forest cake cocktail

ingredients

1 oz (30 mL)   Chambord Royale

12 oz (355 mL)   oatmeal stout (satisfying)

- Pour Chambord Royale into a glass that will hold at least 14 oz (470 mL). Top with a not-too-bitter, not-too-roasty oatmeal stout and serve.

black velvet

This is a classic cocktail known everywhere stout is served. We once met an aficionado who declared that, for him, Christmas morning just wasn't right without a glass of Black Velvet.

ingredients

3 oz (90 mL)   Irish-style stout (satisfying)

2 oz (60 mL)   champagne or dry, sparkling wine

- Pour the stout into a champagne flute. Top with the champagne or other sparkling wine and serve.

cherry ale sangria

We developed this refreshing sangria as a means of serving Quelque Chose—a spiced cherry beer meant to be served mulled—during the hotter months of the year. It quickly became a hit and caused us to sell more of the beer in summer than in winter!

ingredients

26 oz (775 mL)	spiced cherry beer (fruity)
1 oz (30 mL)	Cointreau
1 oz (30 mL)	brandy
3-4	slices of each of orange, lemon, and lime
6 oz (175 mL)	ginger ale
6 oz (175 mL)	soda water

- Place a generous scoop of ice cubes into a 60 oz (1.75 L) pitcher. Pour in beer, Cointreau and brandy, add generous amounts of the sliced fruit, and stir well, mashing up the fruit as you go.
- Top with ginger ale and soda water, adding more ice if necessary to fill the pitcher, and stir again.

makes 40 oz (1.2 L)

coffee and a smoke

You're looking for a balance of coffee and smoke flavours, so depending on the beers chosen, you may have to adjust the proportions in this recipe.

ingredients

12 oz (355 mL)   coffee-flavoured porter or stout (satisfying)

5 oz (150 mL)   smoked malt beer (smoky)

- Pour coffee-flavoured beer into a glass that will hold at least 20 oz (625 mL). Top with smoked malt beer and serve.

compass box cocktail

Compass Box Whisky is a producer of excellent vatted malt whiskies that we hosted one year for a whisky dinner. This was the welcome cocktail, and it went over beautifully with the crowd.

ingredients

1 oz (30 mL)	Compass Box Peat Monster or similarly smoky malt whisky
3 oz (90 mL)	Imperial stout (soothing)
3 dashes	Angostura or Fee Brothers aromatic bitters orange peel twist

- Pour whisky, stout, and bitters into a cocktail shaker filled with ice cubes. Stir gently and strain into a chilled martini glass. Garnish with an orange twist.

green devil

The "devil" in this cocktail is the great Belgian ale, Duvel. You can make it with a different, similarly styled beer but, in our opinion, it won't be quite the same drink.

ingredients

a few drops	absinthe (or Pernod)
1 oz (30 mL)	aromatic gin (such as Martin Miller's gin or Bombay Sapphire)
11 oz (341 mL)	Duvel or other Belgian-style strong golden ale (spicy)

- In a proper Duvel glass or an 18–22 oz (525–650 mL) tulip-shaped glass, swirl absinthe and shake out excess. Add gin and top with Duvel, poured so the foam rises to as near the top of the glass as possible.

maggie's midnight

Created and named for Stephen's wife, this drink incorporates three of her favourite drinks: red wine, Jack Daniels, and stout.

ingredients

2 oz (60 mL)	late bottle vintage (LBV) port wine
1/2 oz (15 mL)	Jack Daniels or other American whiskey
12 oz (355 mL)	Imperial stout (soothing)

• Pour port and Jack Daniels into a glass will hold at least 16 oz (500 mL). Top with stout and serve.

mimosa bianco

A refreshing afternoon sipper.

ingredients

8 oz (235 mL)	Belgian-style wheat beer (quenching)
4 oz (125 mL)	freshly squeezed orange juice

• Combine beer and orange juice in a glass that will hold at least 14 oz (470 mL) and serve.

acknowledgements

A book like this requires the talents of so many people and I've been very fortunate to be surrounded by some great ones. Thank you Kathleen McGinn, my business partner and friend, for your constant support; Michelle Usprech for organizing me; Carol Harrison, you are the best editor I've ever known; Michael Mouland, you are the guy who brought it all together; Alison Carr and Martin Gould for capturing the essence; and Mike McColl for his incomparable photography. I am also truly grateful to Jordan Fenn without whom we would never have had this book: thanks for eating at the restaurant so often. Last, I'd like to bow to the many brewmasters who challenge themselves everyday to produce so many incredible brews.

—Brian

The proverbial wind beneath my wings is my lovely wife, Maggie, without whom I would be nowhere: thank you, sweetheart. My thanks also go to my parents for raising a pretty good kid; my co-author and friend, Brian, for inflaming all those who surround you with your passion for great food; my many editors and publishers, both book and magazine, for allowing me to pursue this crazy career; and all the diverse souls who make the brewing industry such a great place to be. Cheers to you all!

—Stephen

index